Requiem Rising

Original Compositions by:
Bill Walker

ISBN: 979-8-9890167-4-7

www.billwalkercomposer.com

BWMP

Published by
Bill Walker Music Publishing

8227 S 70th Dr
Laveen, AZ 85339

All interior information and layout as well as front and back cover designs by Bill Walker.
Artwork for the cover was created by prompts input into Adobe Firefly.

Printed in the United States of America

Dive into a symphony of emotions with ***Requiem Rising***, a captivating collection of original compositions. This book presents a beautiful tapestry of music that transitions from darkness to light, embodying a profound passage through life's most intimate emotional landscapes. Embark on a transcendent experience where each note is a step towards rediscovery, resilience, and the ultimate triumph of the human spirit.

Featured Compositions:

1. **Alone, Lost** is written in F minor and is an evocative piece spanning just four pages. It captures the essence of solitude and the profound feeling of being lost, whether physically or internally. Through a gradual progression, the music unfolds to a resolution that offers a sense of direction and a glimmer of hope.

2. **Drifting Away** is a piece in E minor that transitions to D minor during its seven pages. It meanders through a journey devoid of direction or a clear destination, with sections of thoughtful contemplation interspersed with hurried passages, reflecting a mild sense of panic. After transitioning to D minor, the piece shifts into a phase of introspection, leaving the outcome and destination open to interpretation inviting individuals to discern their own conclusions.

3. **Forbidden Desires**, written in F minor is compelling and evokes the allure and intrigue of something forbidden over its eight pages. It features a middle section that vividly portrays the sensation of being chased or chasing after, whether physically or mentally, inviting listeners to choose their interpretation. The conclusion conveys a sense of resignation, representing either the surrender to or resistance of one's forbidden desires, leaving the emotional resolution up to the individual's perspective.

4. **Soulful Exploration** is composed in C minor and embarks the listener on a profound journey to explore the depths of their soul throughout its seven pages. It begins with a somber theme that invites introspection. As subsequent themes weave between uncertainty and drive, the piece mirrors the process of examining one's values to determine what truly matters. The unpredictable ending, marked by unexpected dissonance, resolves swiftly into a harmonious conclusion, leading the listener to exactly where they are meant to be.

5. **Traversing the Realm of Darkness**, a composition in C-sharp minor comprising six pages, immerses the listener in a shadowy landscape with an unyielding sense of determination. This piece conveys the relentless drive to persevere through the darkest of times, capturing the essence of persistence and resilience. The rhythmic intensity and powerful motifs guide one through the obscurity, emphasizing the unwavering resolve to press on despite the overwhelming challenges.

6. **Beyond the Icy Veil** is a thrilling journey through a frozen, mysterious realm. This nine-page piece begins in G minor and navigates the beauty of the ice with its hidden dangers. The transition to C minor reinforces the awe and hazard of venturing into an enchanting, icy landscape, unaware of the spectacular wonders and challenges that await beyond the icy barrier.

7. **Into the Void** an eight-page piece in A minor, captures the essence of venturing into the unknown realms of space, where the boundaries of time and existence blur. The journey isn't about reaching a destination but exploring the mysterious in-between spaces. The fading conclusion leaves listeners pondering whether the traveler returns to normalcy or disappears into the cosmos, leaving their fate an open mystery.

8. **Final Rites** in E minor immerses you in a retro-futuristic world, where '80s sci-fi meets pensive introspection. Over seven pages mysterious bass rhythms pulse like a dystopian heartbeat, transitioning to a contemplative melody before climaxing in a dramatic, abrupt end. This piece evokes neon-lit cityscapes and the continued tension of a hero's journey through a shadowy future.

9. **Threads of Time** in just six pages, weaves life's moments into a rich tapestry, beginning with thoughts of joy and contentment. It transitions through challenging, melancholic periods marked by sad determination. The piece ultimately returns to a light and whimsical conclusion, reminding us that there is hope even in our darkest periods. Through determination, happier endings are within reach.

10. **The Light Through the Shadows** is a journey of hope and determination. This piece navigates through three different key signatures within its eight pages, each filled with a sense of resolve. The steady rhythm in the left hand symbolizes unwavering perseverance, driving the melody forward even in the face of adversity. It captures the essence of finding clarity and strength amidst life's challenges.

11. **Serenity's Storm** is a thrilling composition in D minor that blends intense moments with serene interludes over twelve pages. *Serenity's Storm* embodies the excitement of moving forward. The piece is both invigorating to play and to listen to, capturing the sense of determination amidst the tempest. With rhythmic drive, it propels through challenges while offering brief pauses to catch one's breath, symbolizing the balance between turmoil and tranquility.

12. **For Angie** is an eight-page, heartfelt, and pensive composition in A minor named for my wife Angie. This piece captures an intense sense of longing and introspection. Its melody resonates deeply with my wife's tender emotions and offers a soulful reflection for all individuals - pianists and listeners alike.

Discover the deeply emotional and transformative journey of *Requiem Rising*. Each piece invites you to explore the depths of human experience, offering both challenge and solace, inspiring people everywhere to connect with this music in a profoundly personal way.

Happy playing!

Bill Walker

Requiem Rising

TABLE OF CONTENTS

Alone, Lost

Adagio (♩ = 72)

Music by Bill Walker

With pedal

(R.H.)

8vb

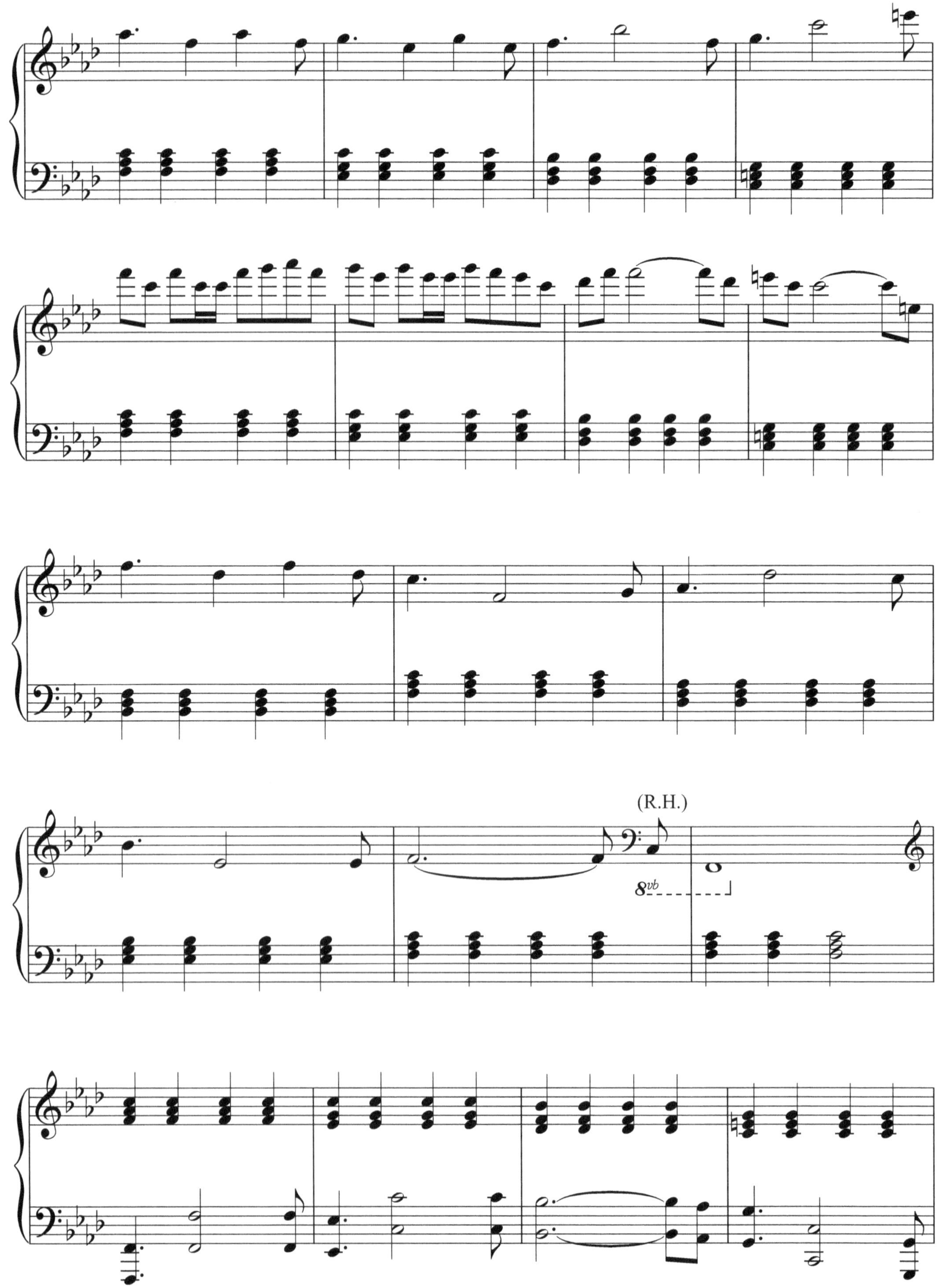
(R.H.)
8vb

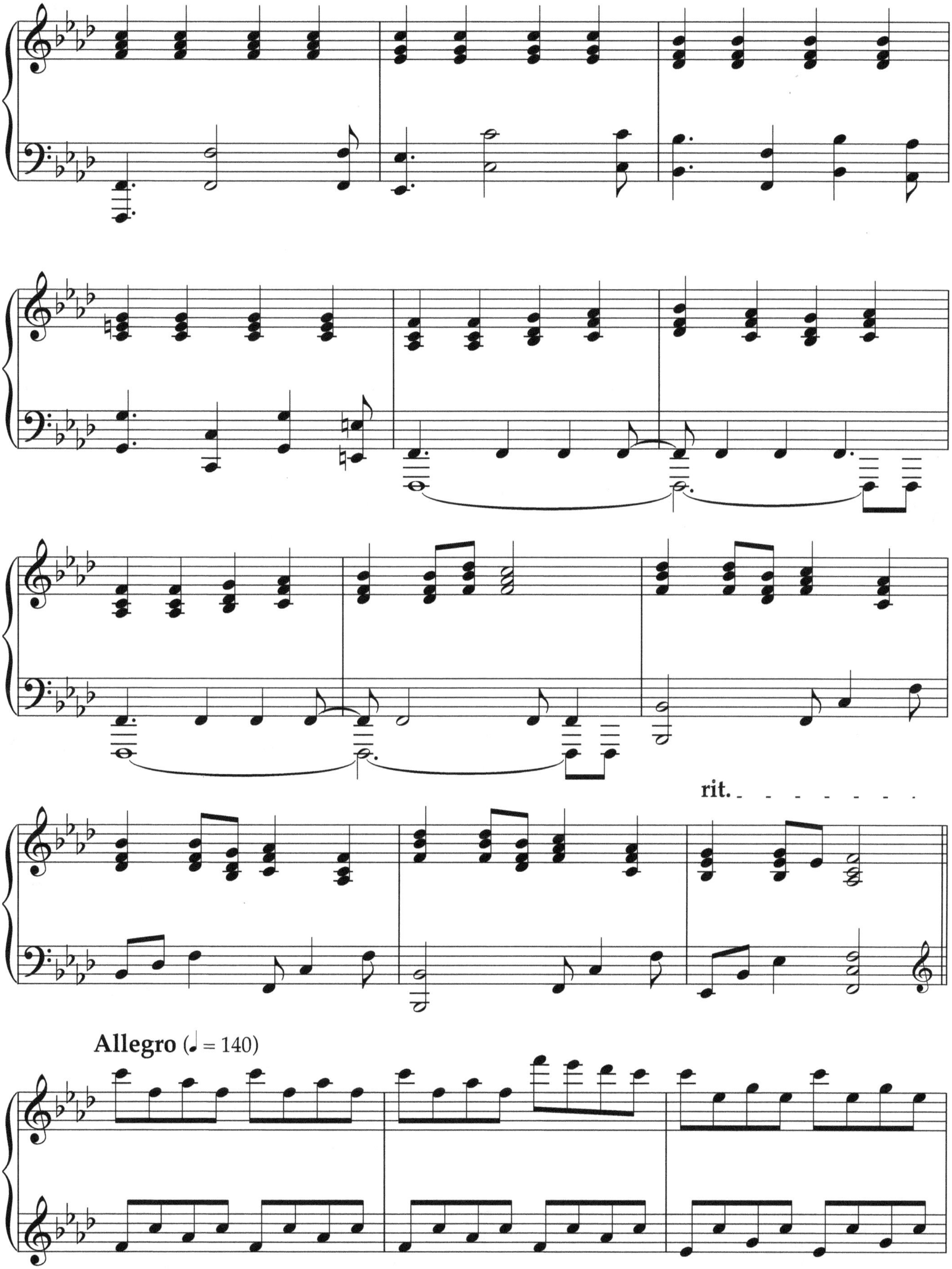
rit.
Allegro (♩ = 140)

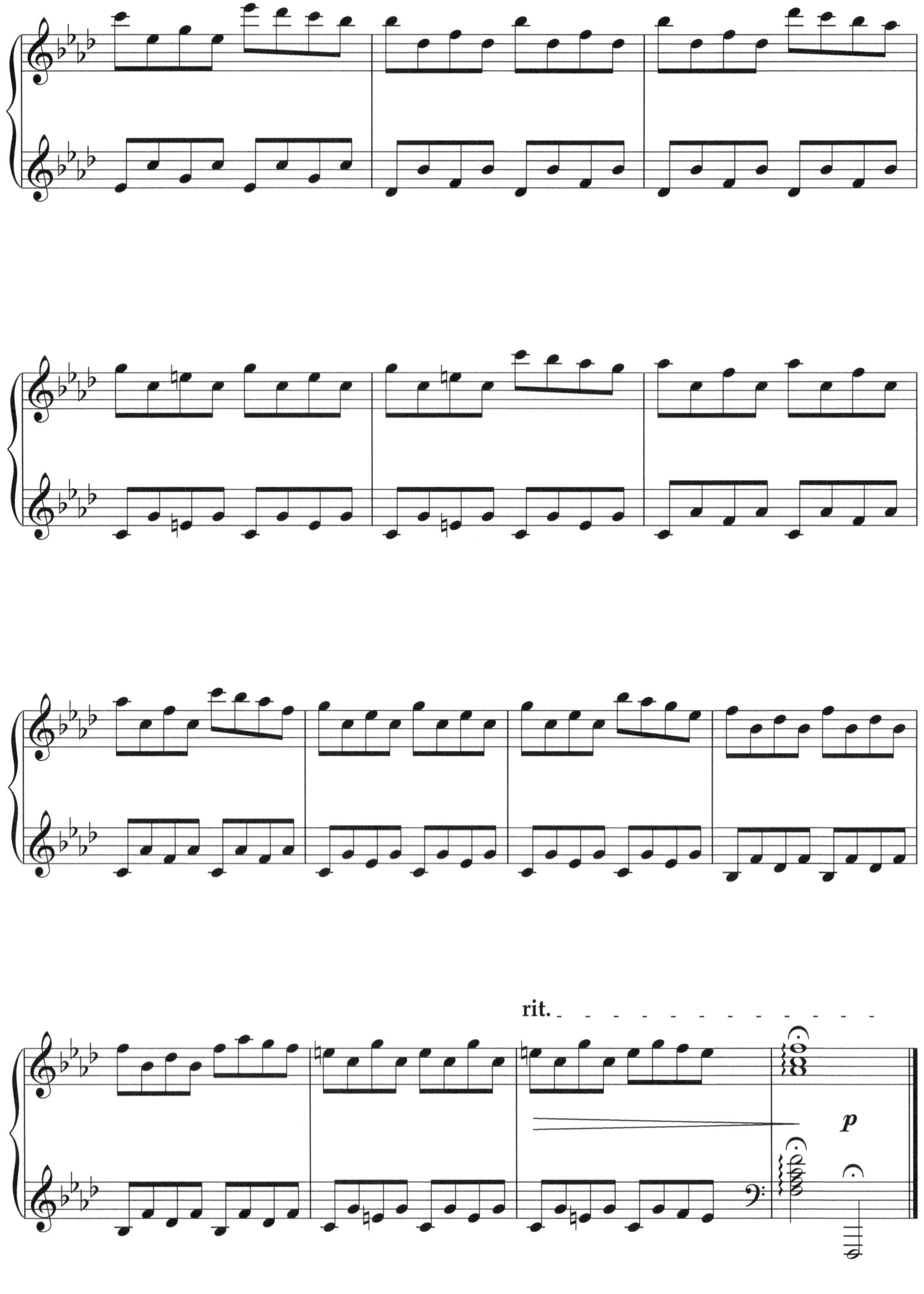
rit.
p

Drifting Away

Music by Bill Walker

Andante Moderato (♩ = 108)

A tempo (♩ = 108)

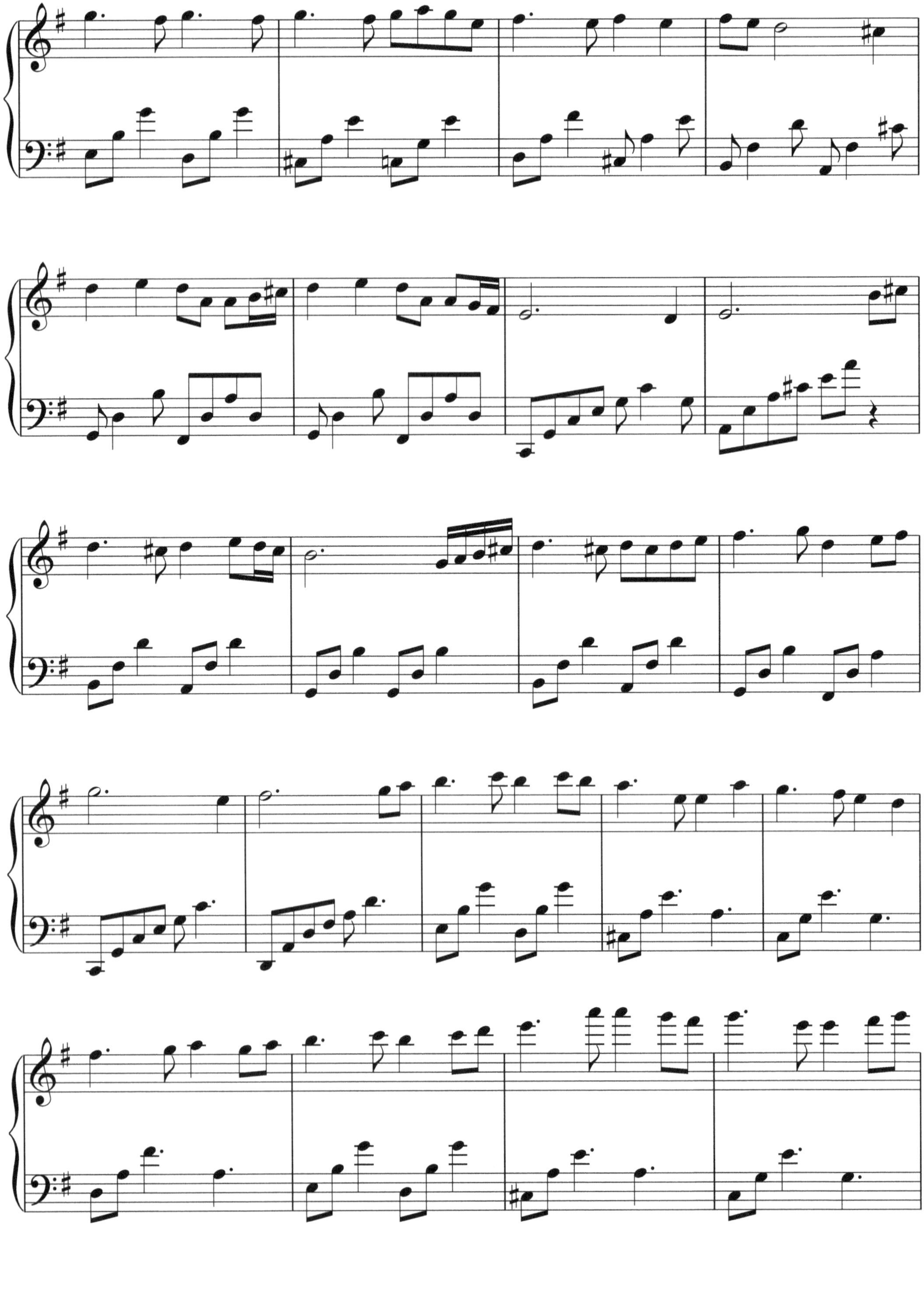

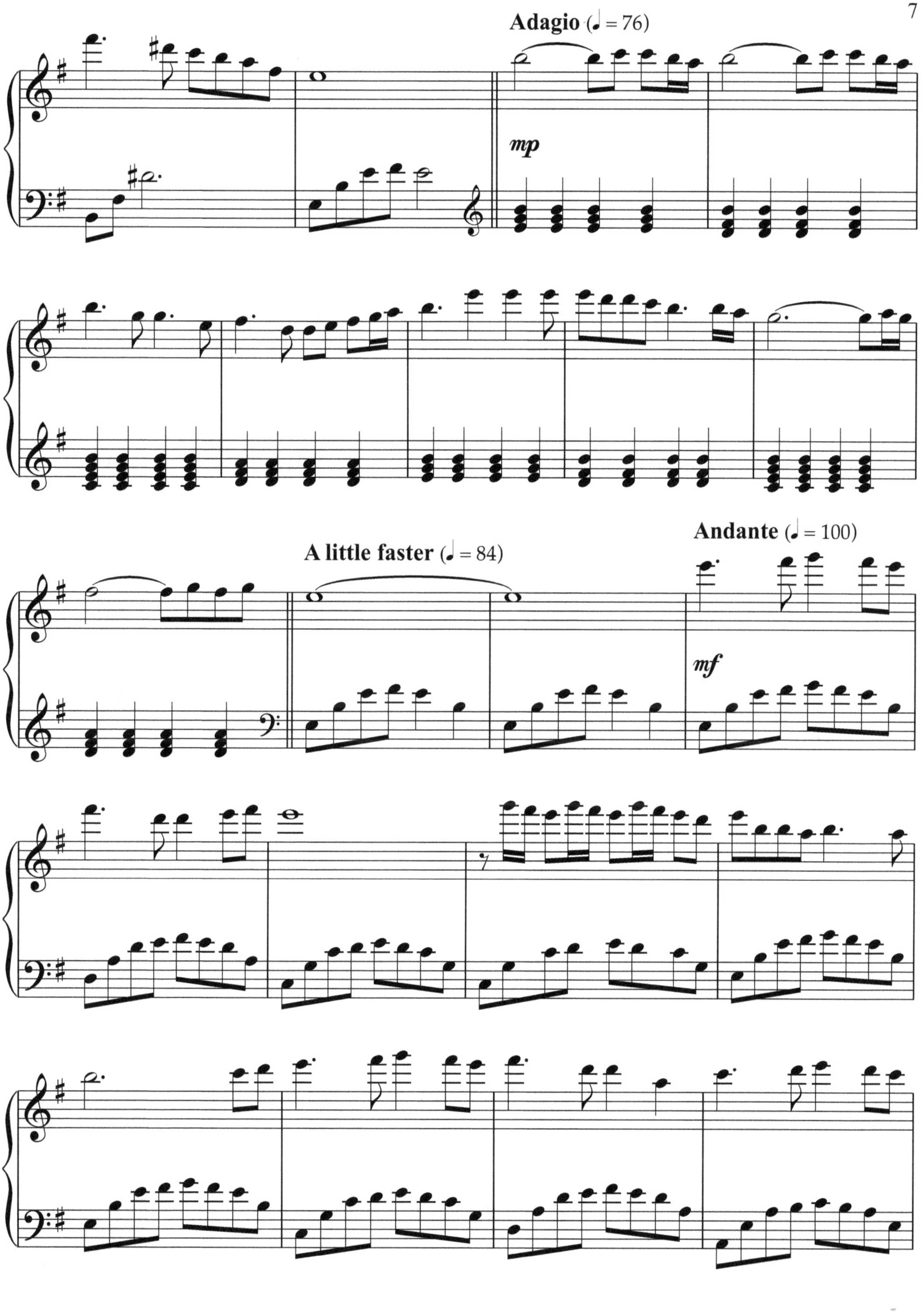
Adagio (♩ = 76)
mp
A little faster (♩ = 84)
Andante (♩ = 100)
mf

A little slower ($\textltimes$ = 92)

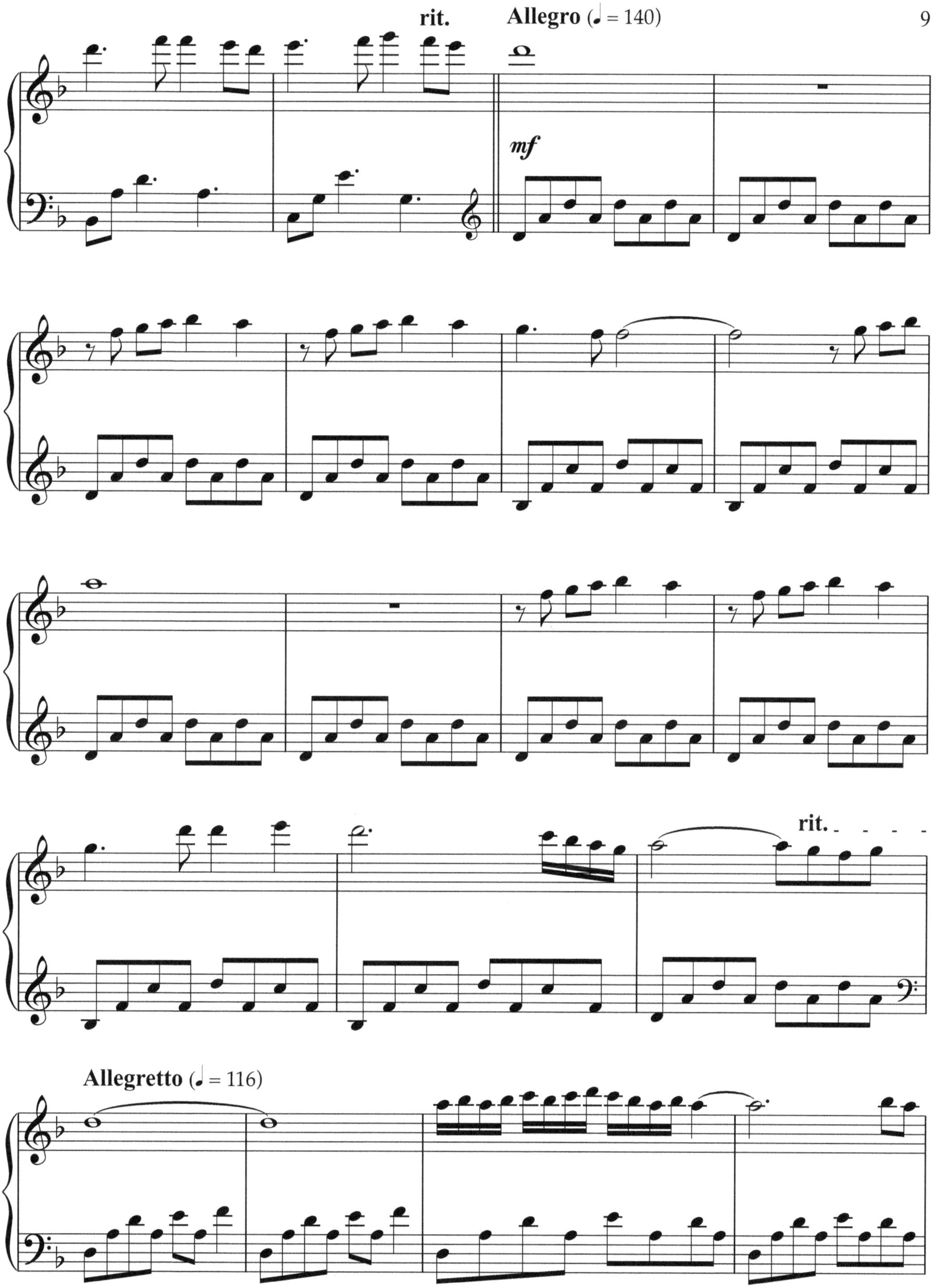
rit.
Allegro (♩ = 140)
mf
rit.
Allegretto (♩ = 116)

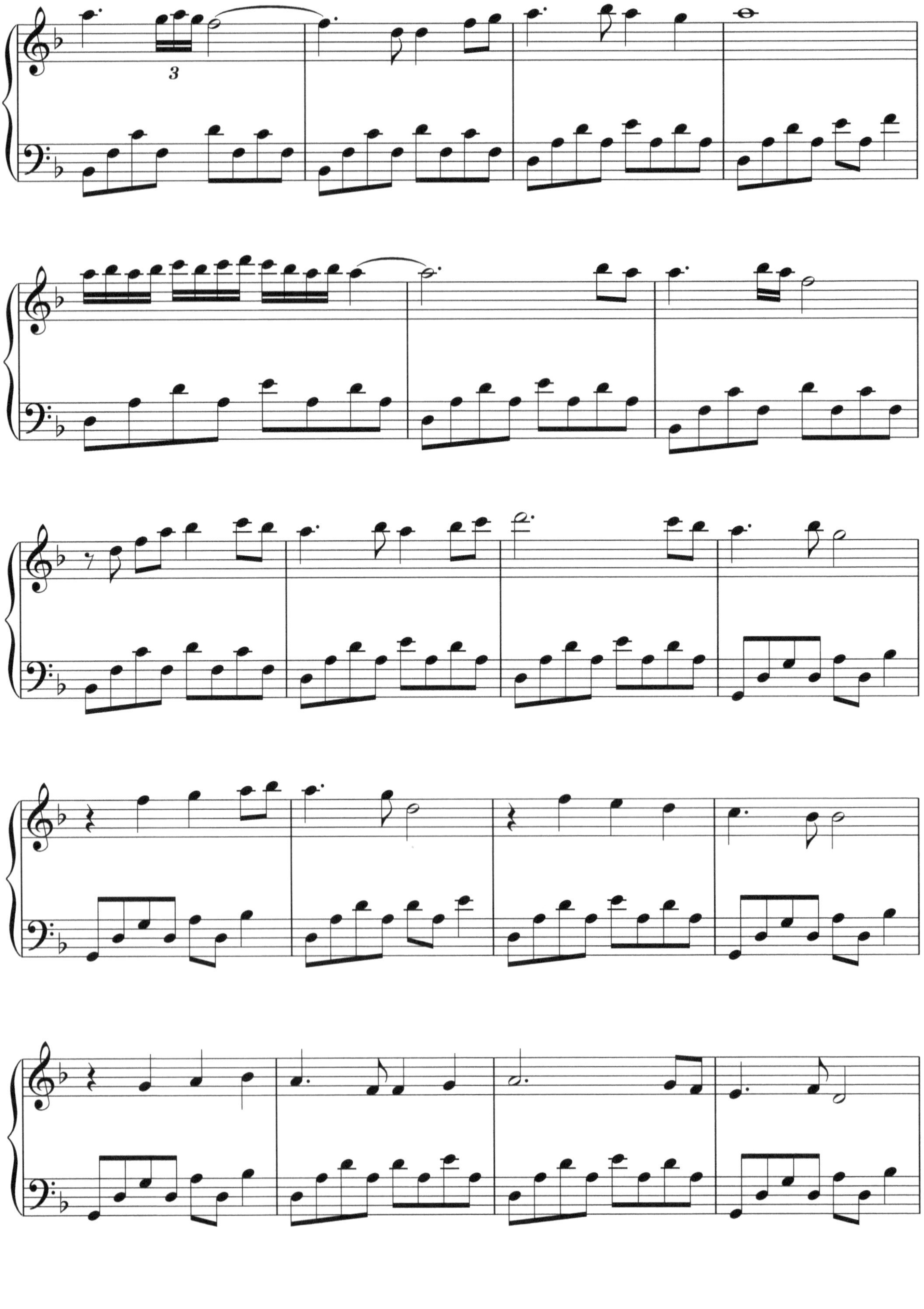
3

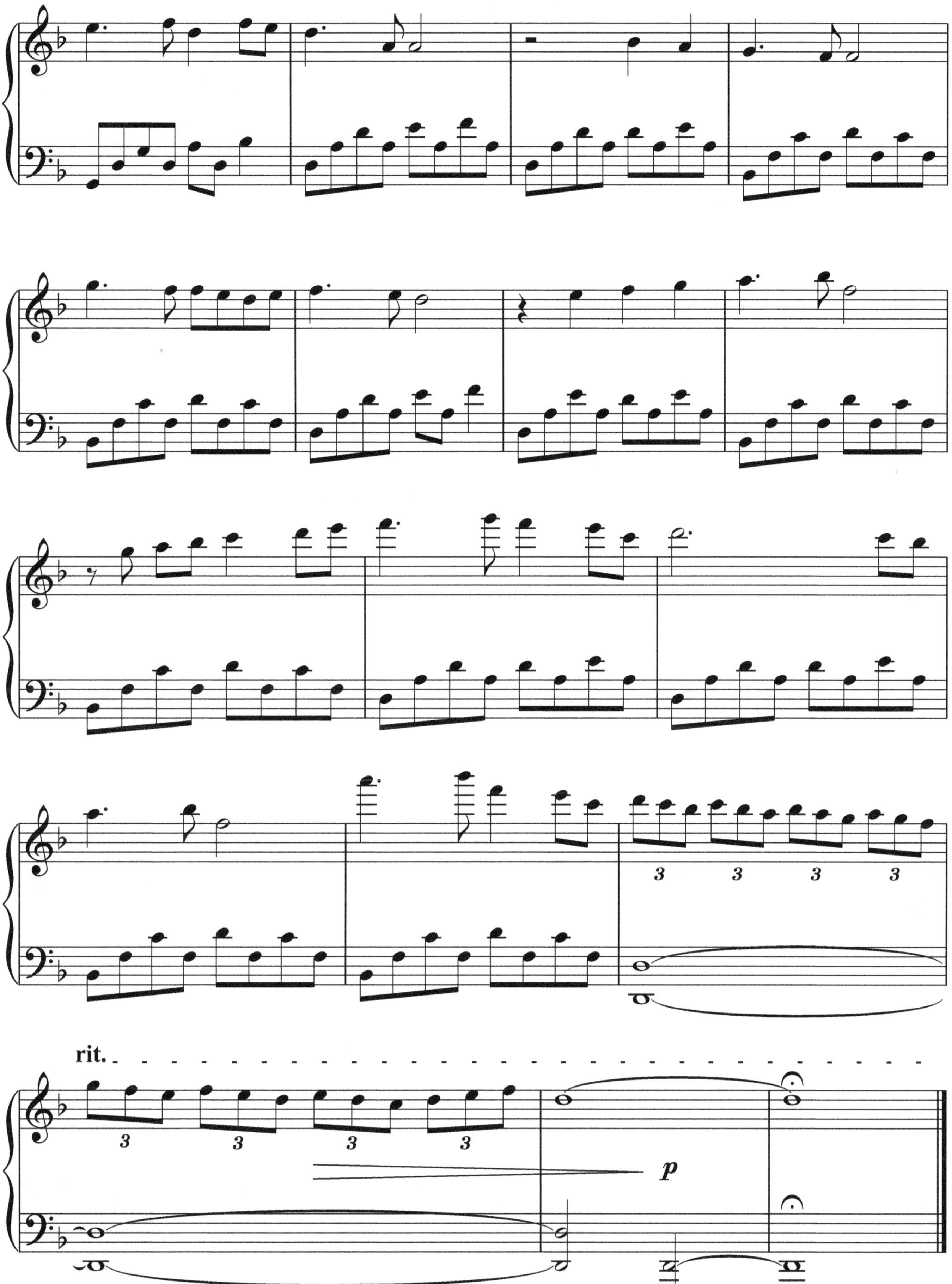
3
3
3
3
rit.
3
3
3
3
p

Forbidden Desires

Music by Bill Walker

Moderato (♩ = 112)

With pedal

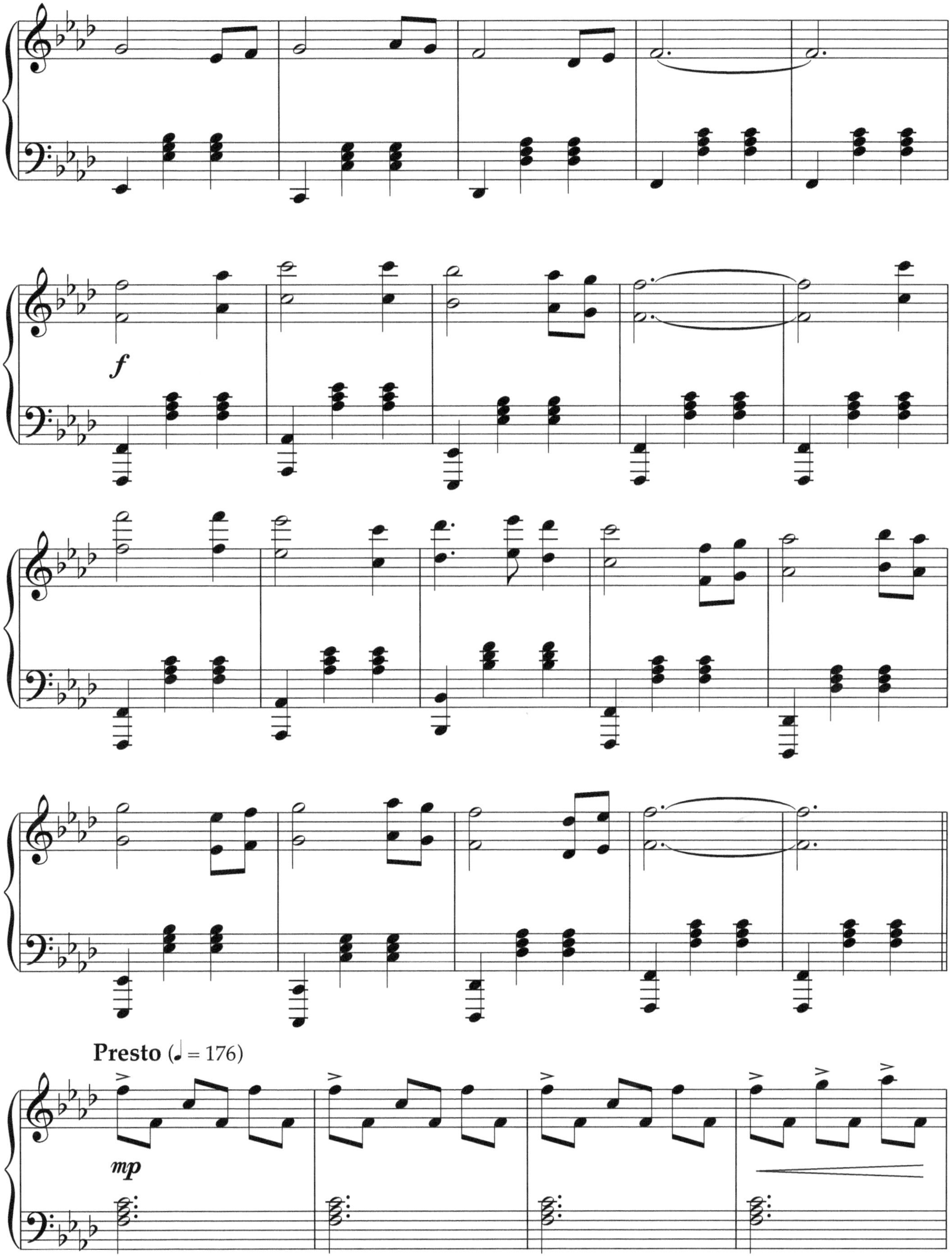
f
Presto (♩ = 176)
mp

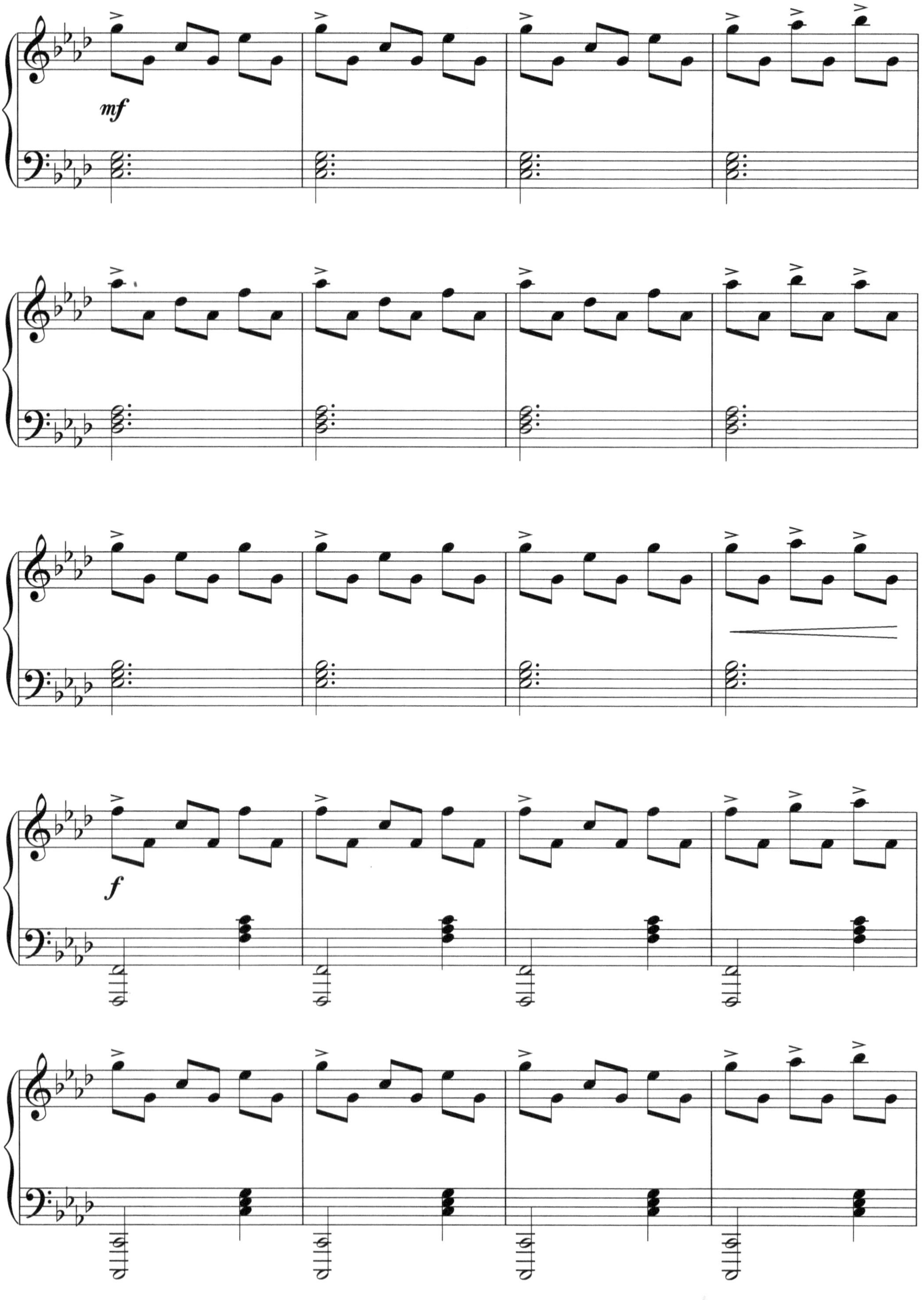
mf
f

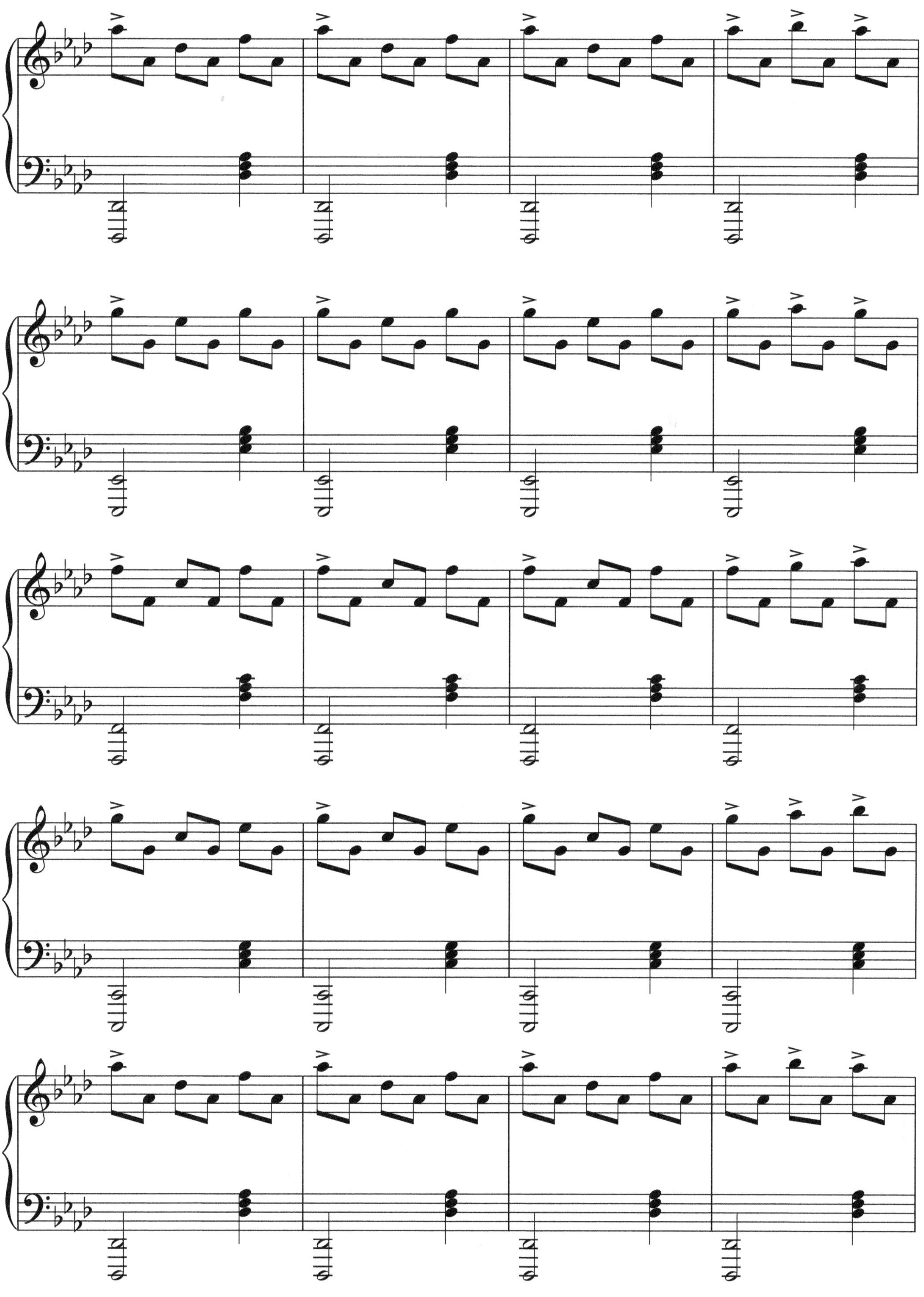

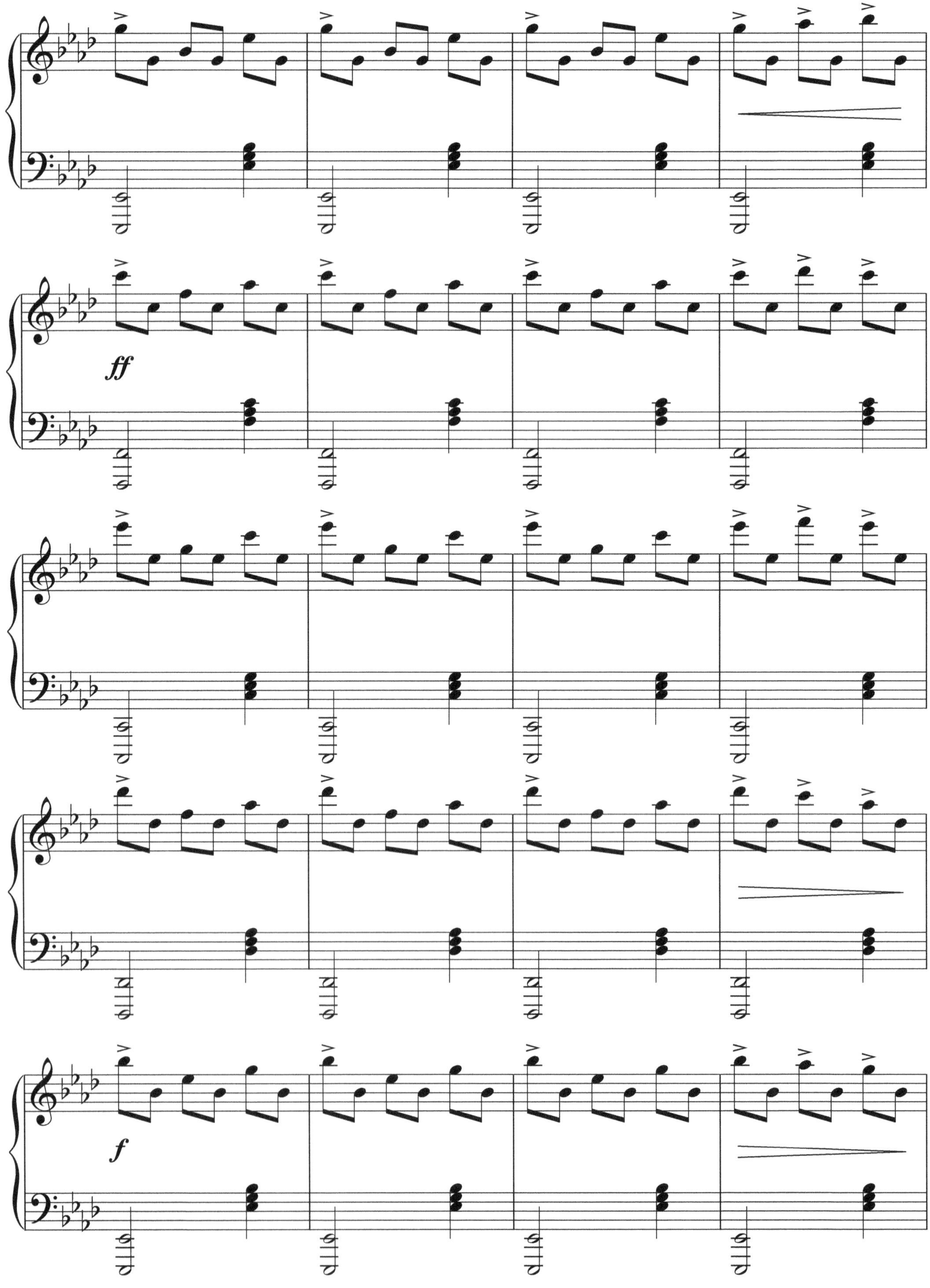
ff
f

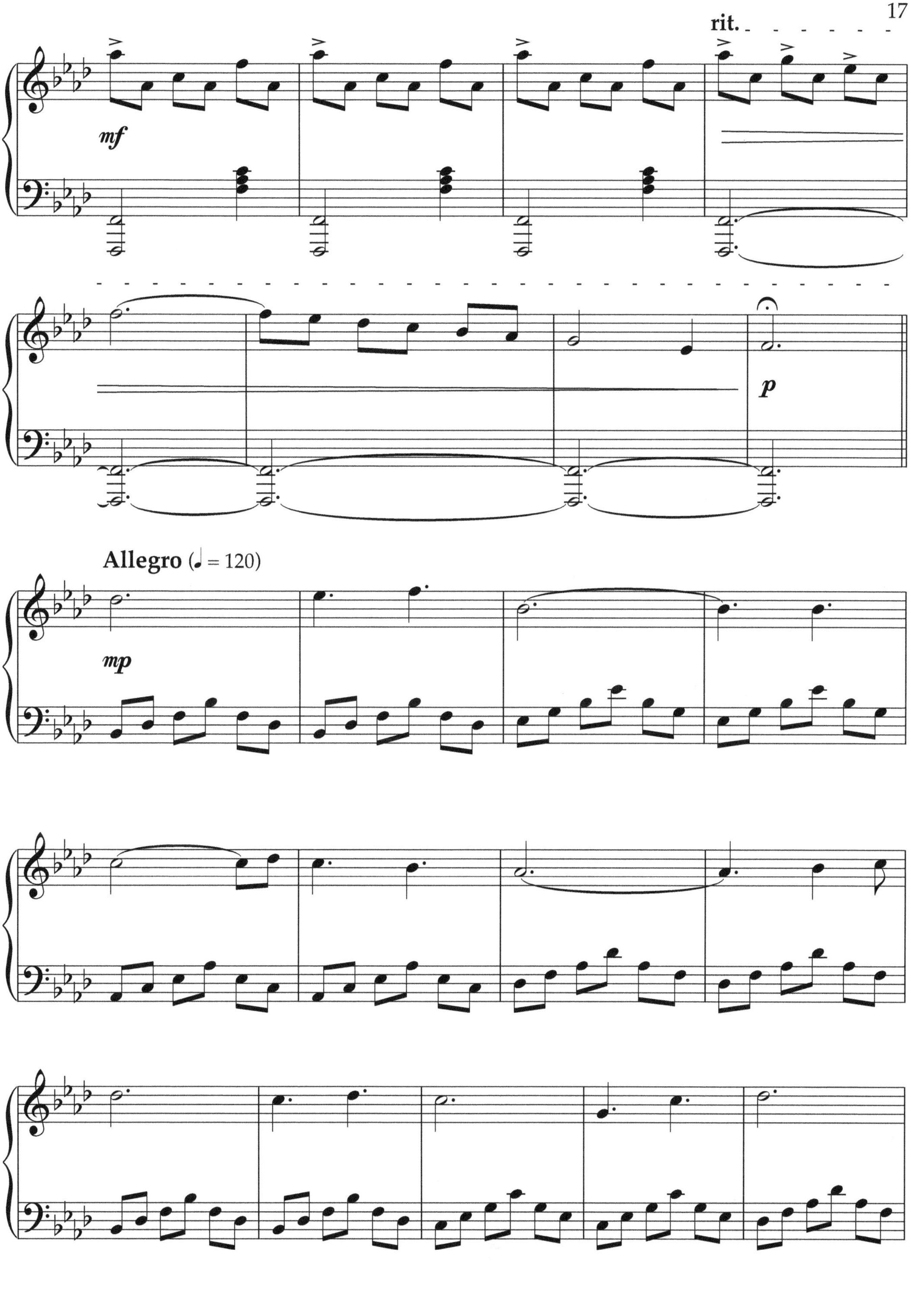
rit.
mf
p
Allegro (♩ = 120)
mp

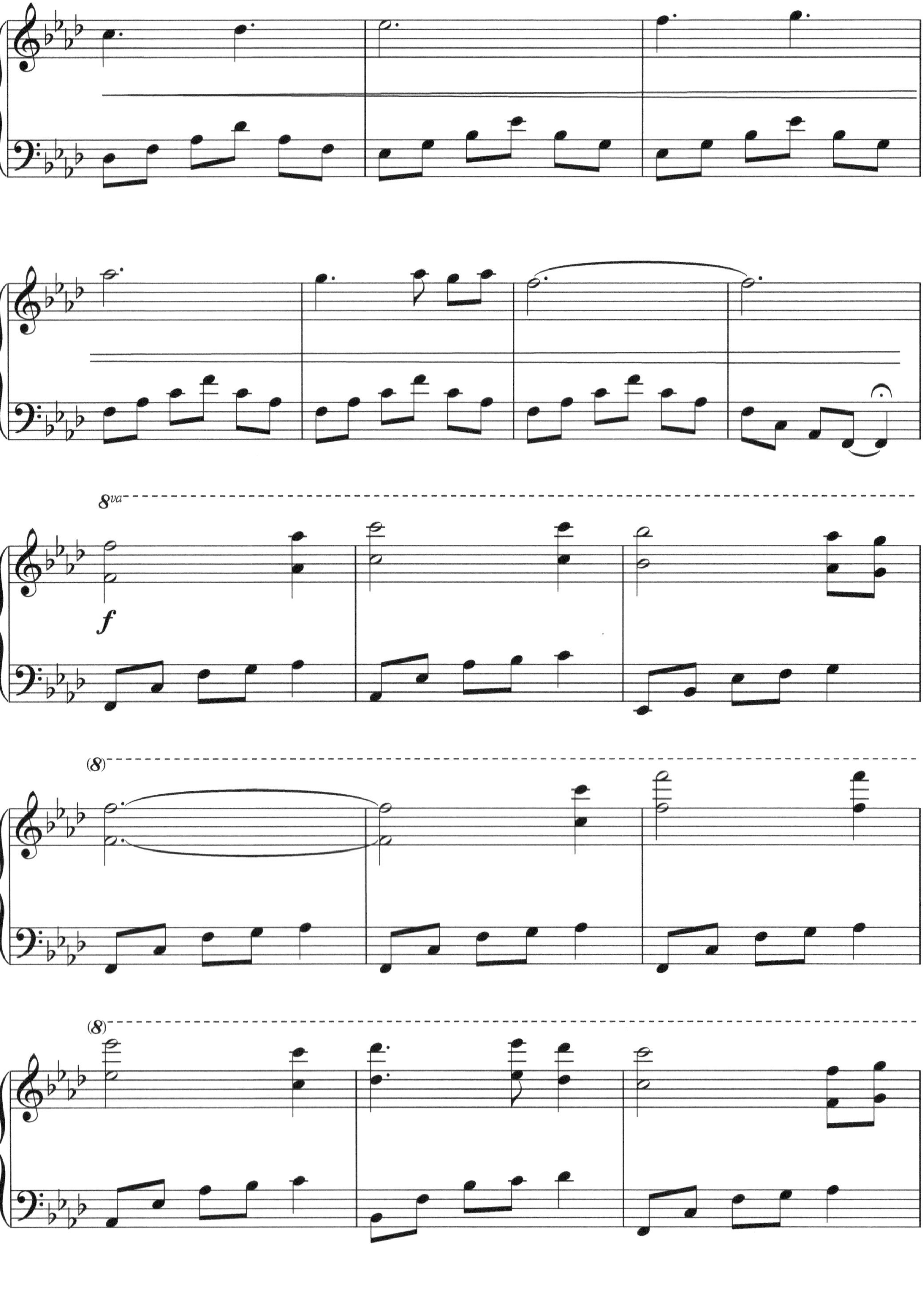
8va
f
(8)
(8)

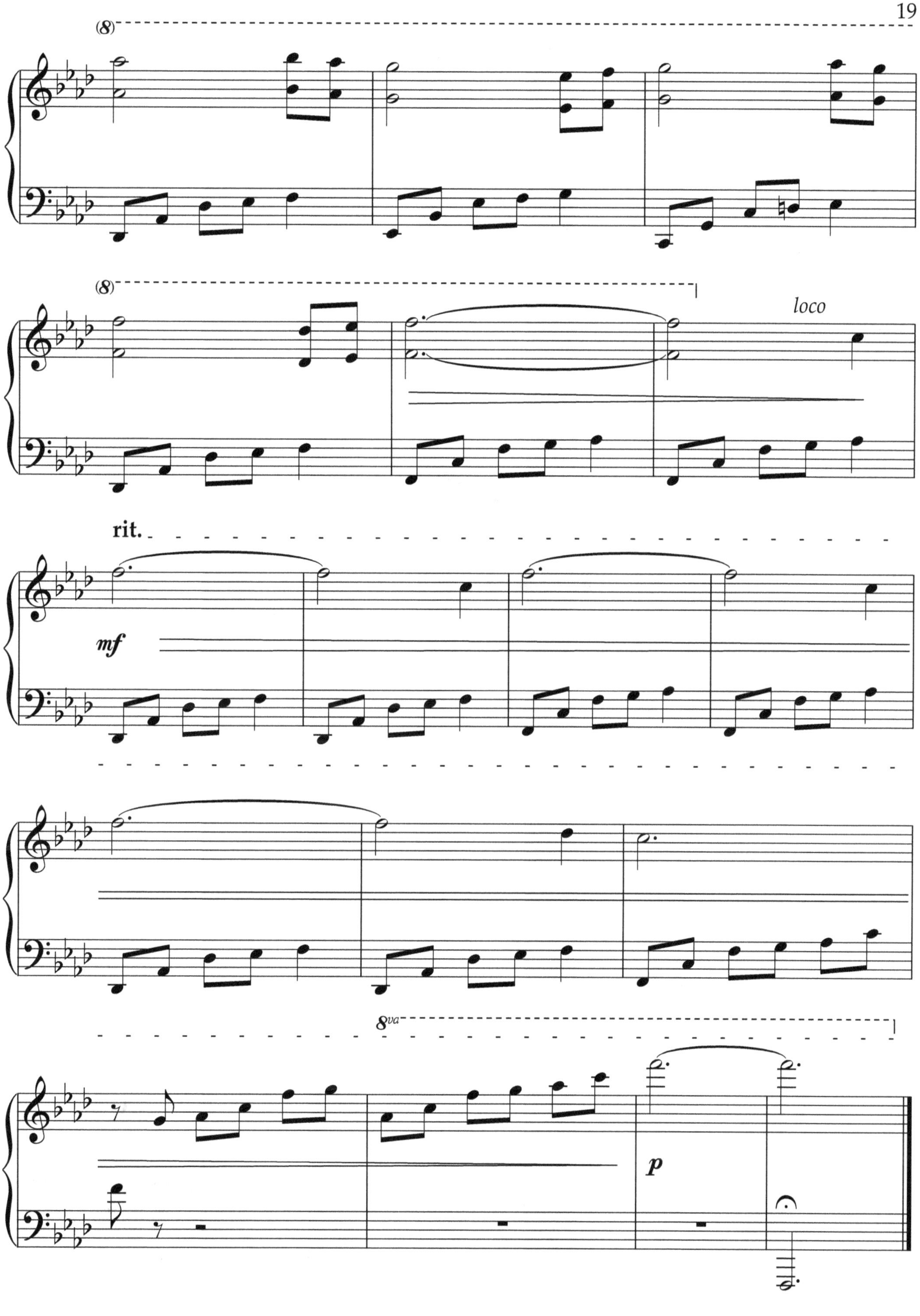
(8)
(8)
loco
rit.
mf
8va
p

Soulful Exploration

Music by Bill Walker

Tempo primo (♩ = 84)

Allegro (♩ = 144)

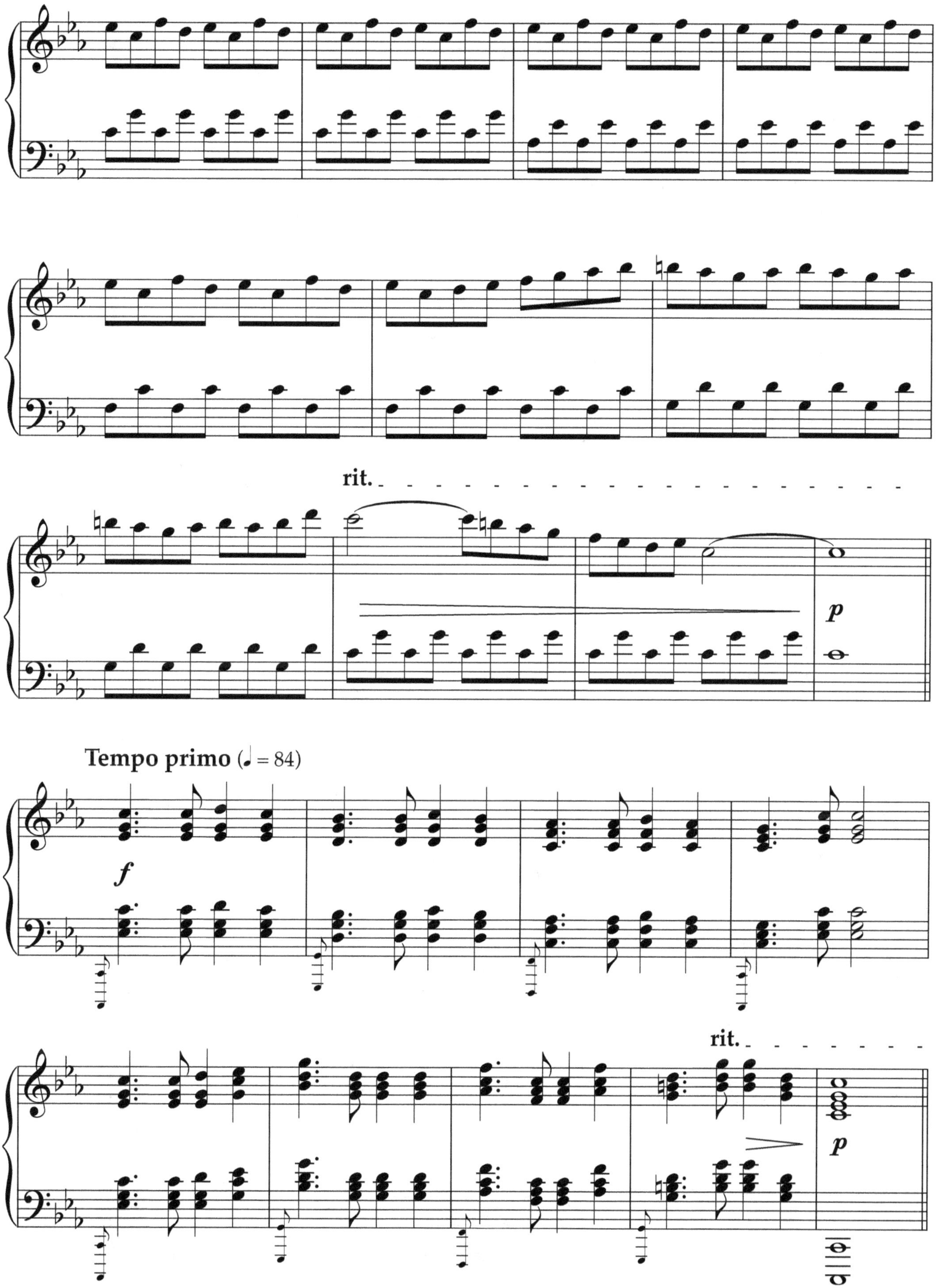
rit.
p
Tempo primo (♩ = 84)
f
rit.
p

Molto Allegro (♩ = 160)

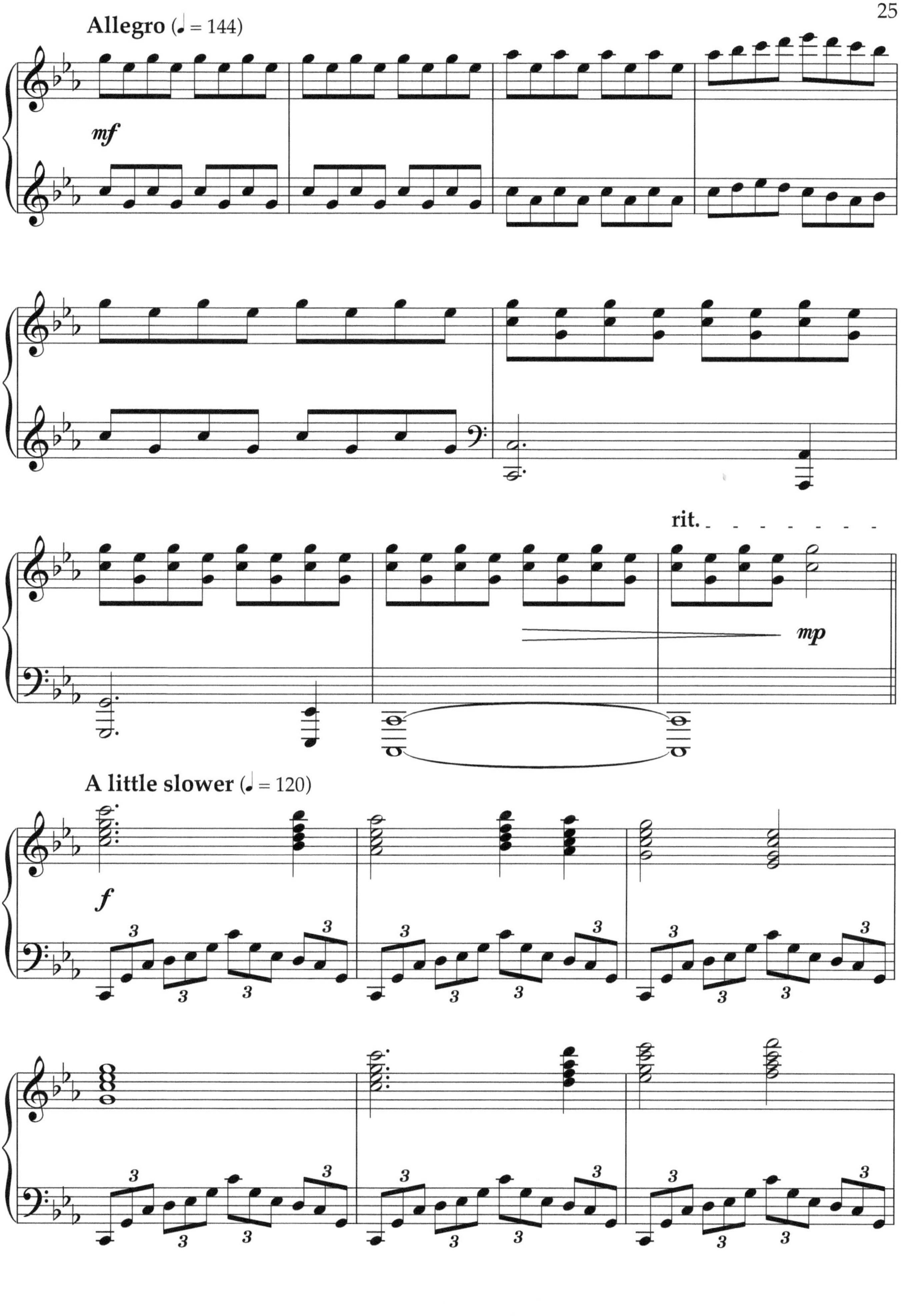
Allegro (♩ = 144)
mf
rit.
mp
A little slower (♩ = 120)
f
3

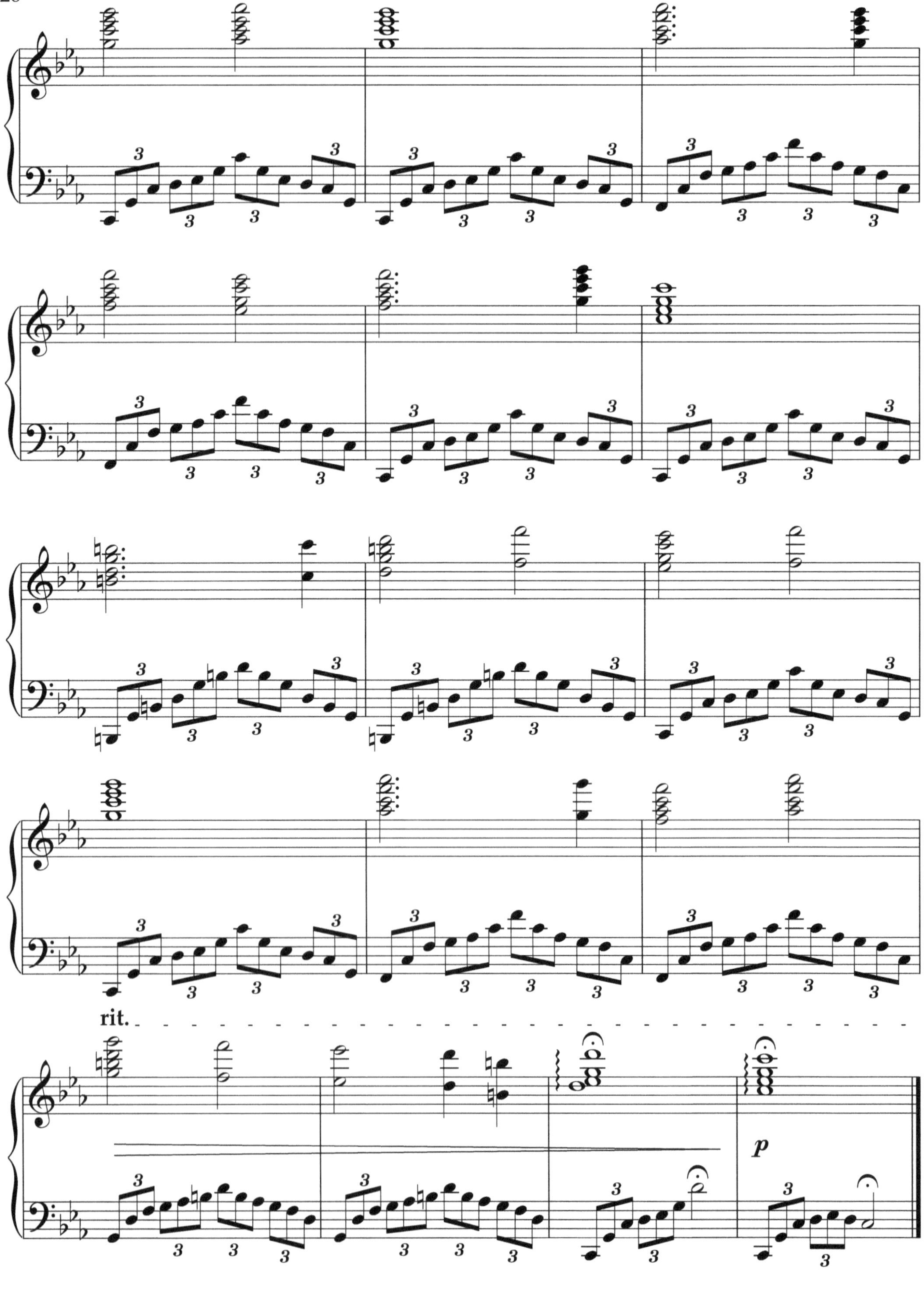
rit.
p

Traversing the Realm of Darkness

Music by Bill Walker

Continually moving forward (♩ = 80)

With pedal

A tempo (♩ = 80)

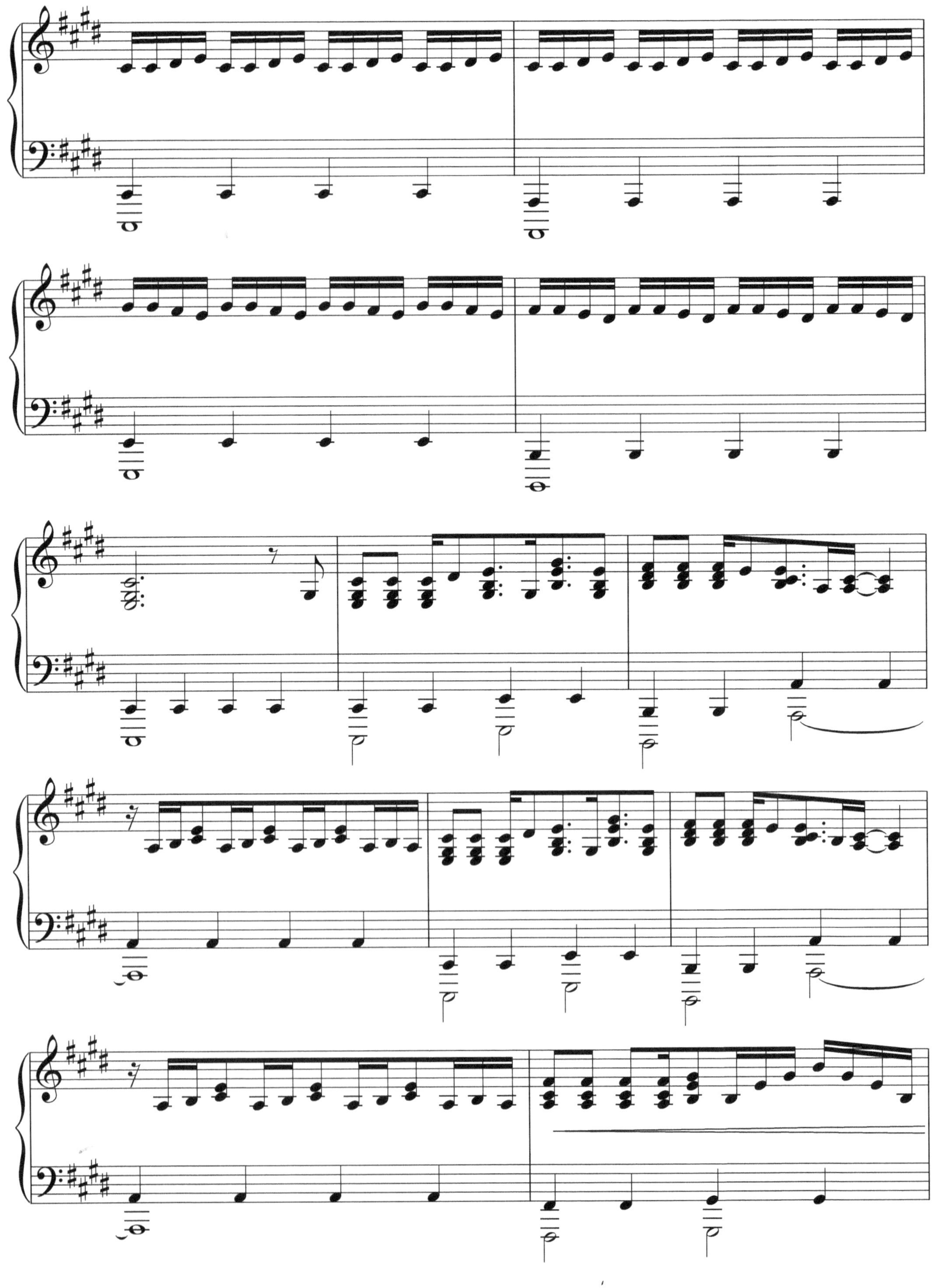

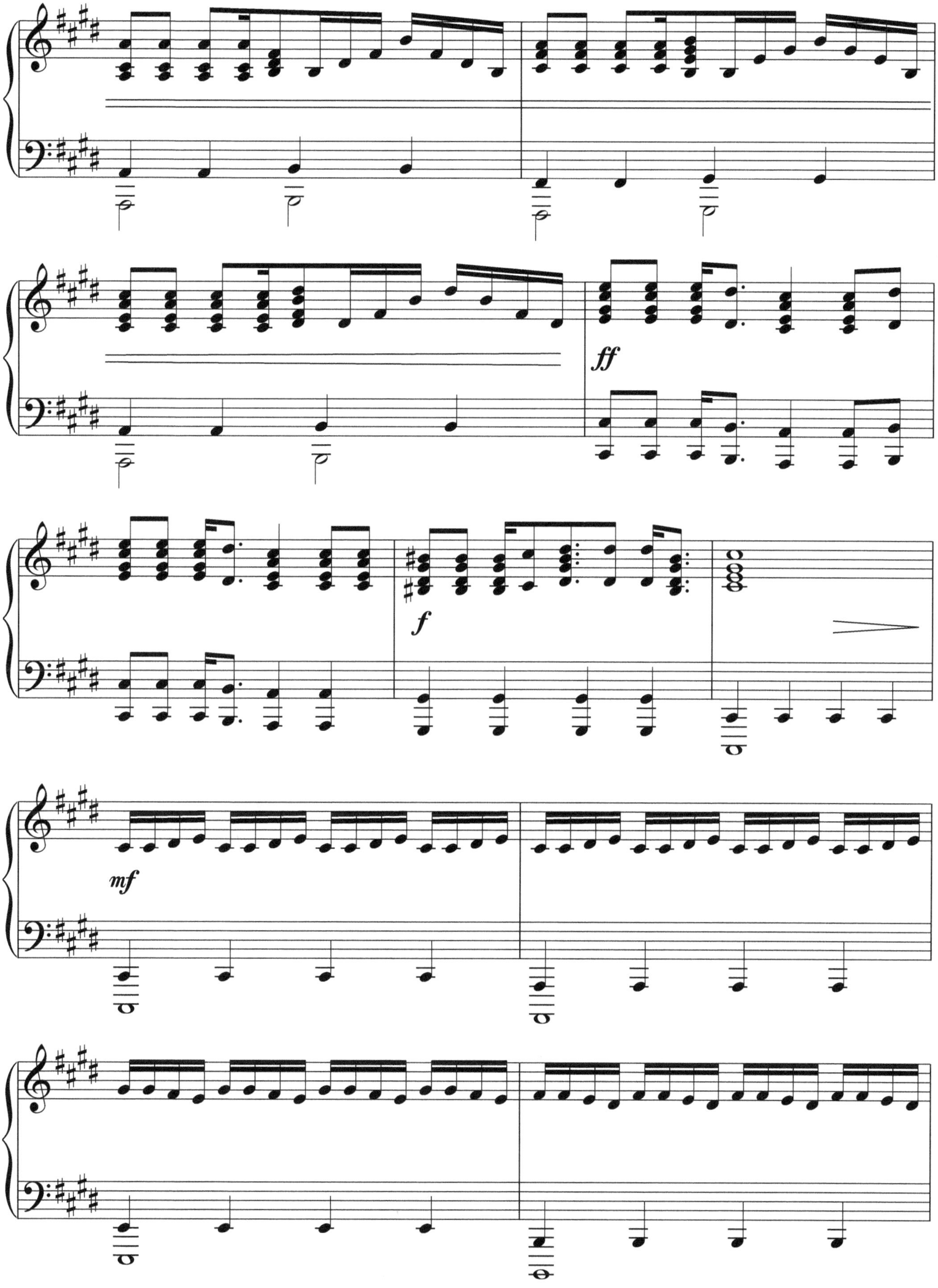
ff
f
mf

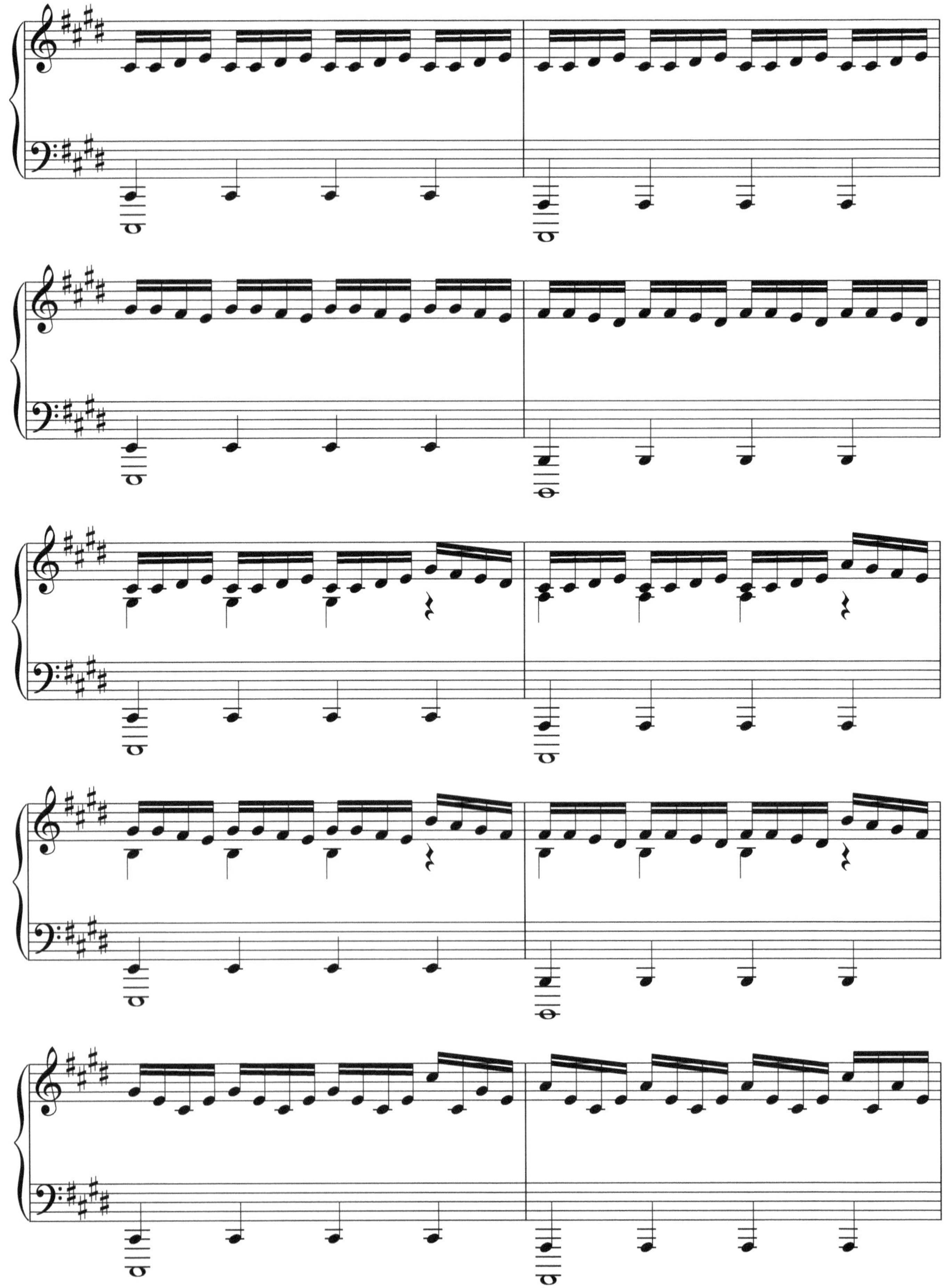

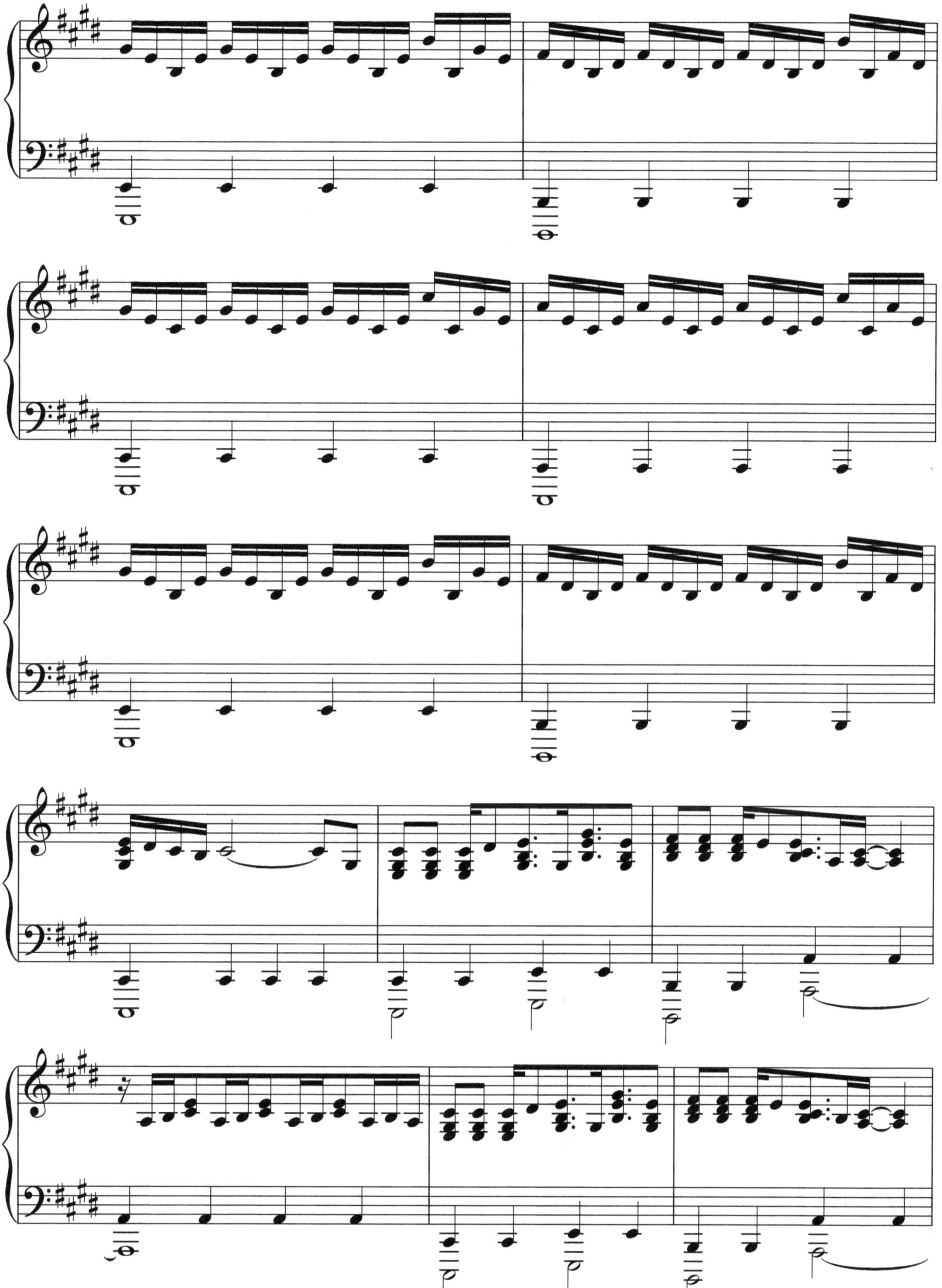

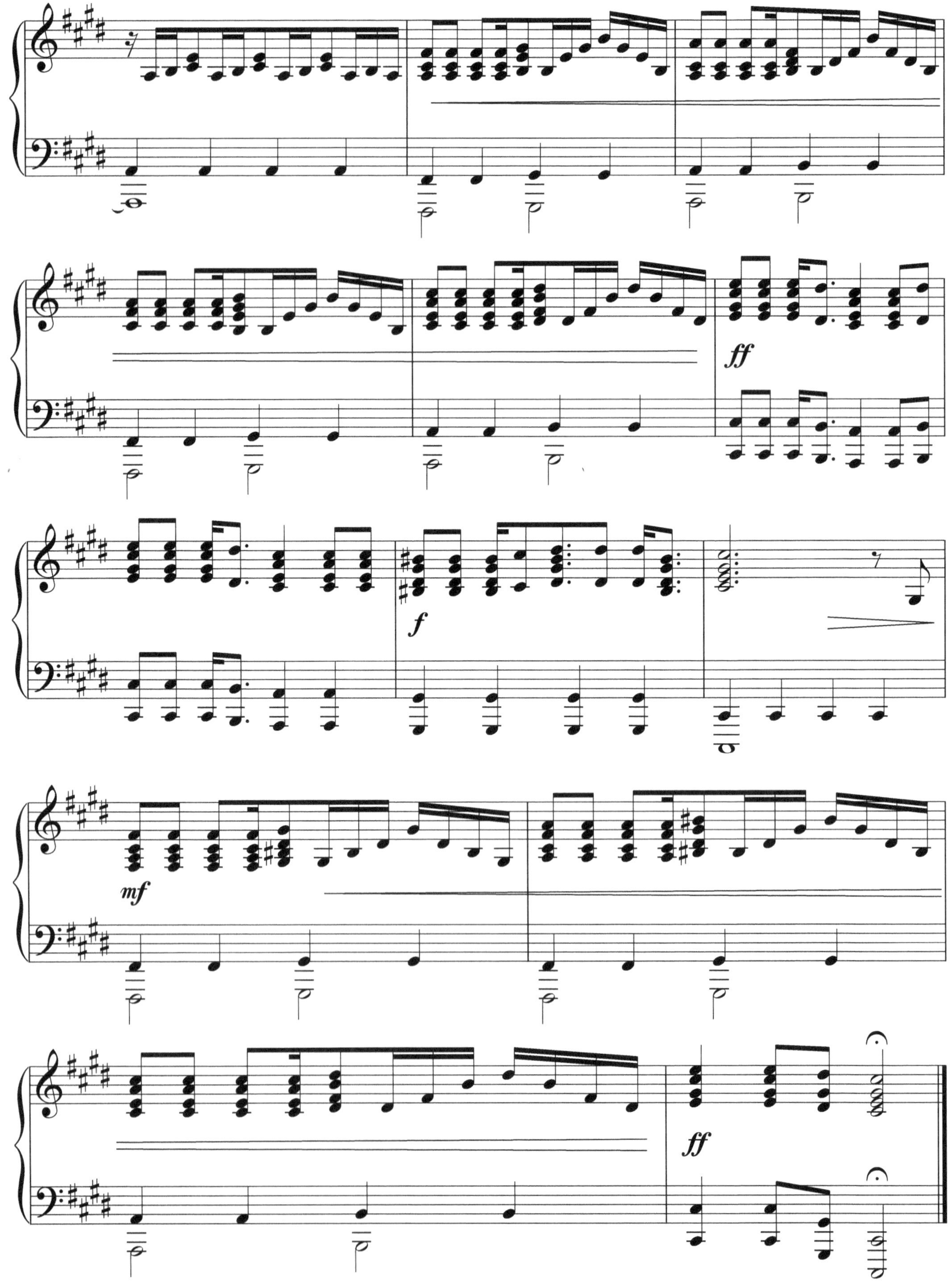
ff
f
mf
ff

Beyond the Icy Veil

Flowing ($\quarternote = 120$)

Music by Bill Walker

With pedal

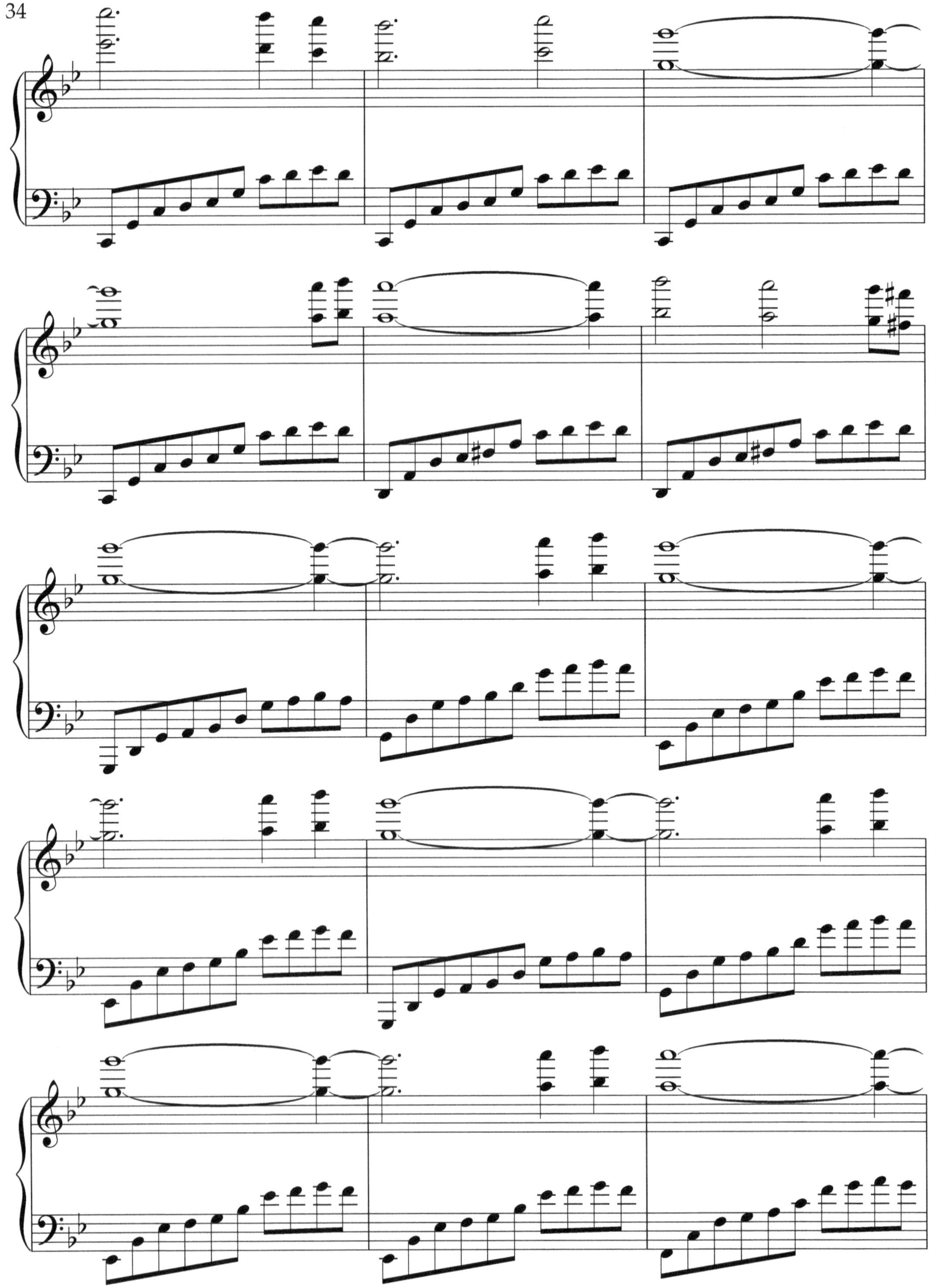

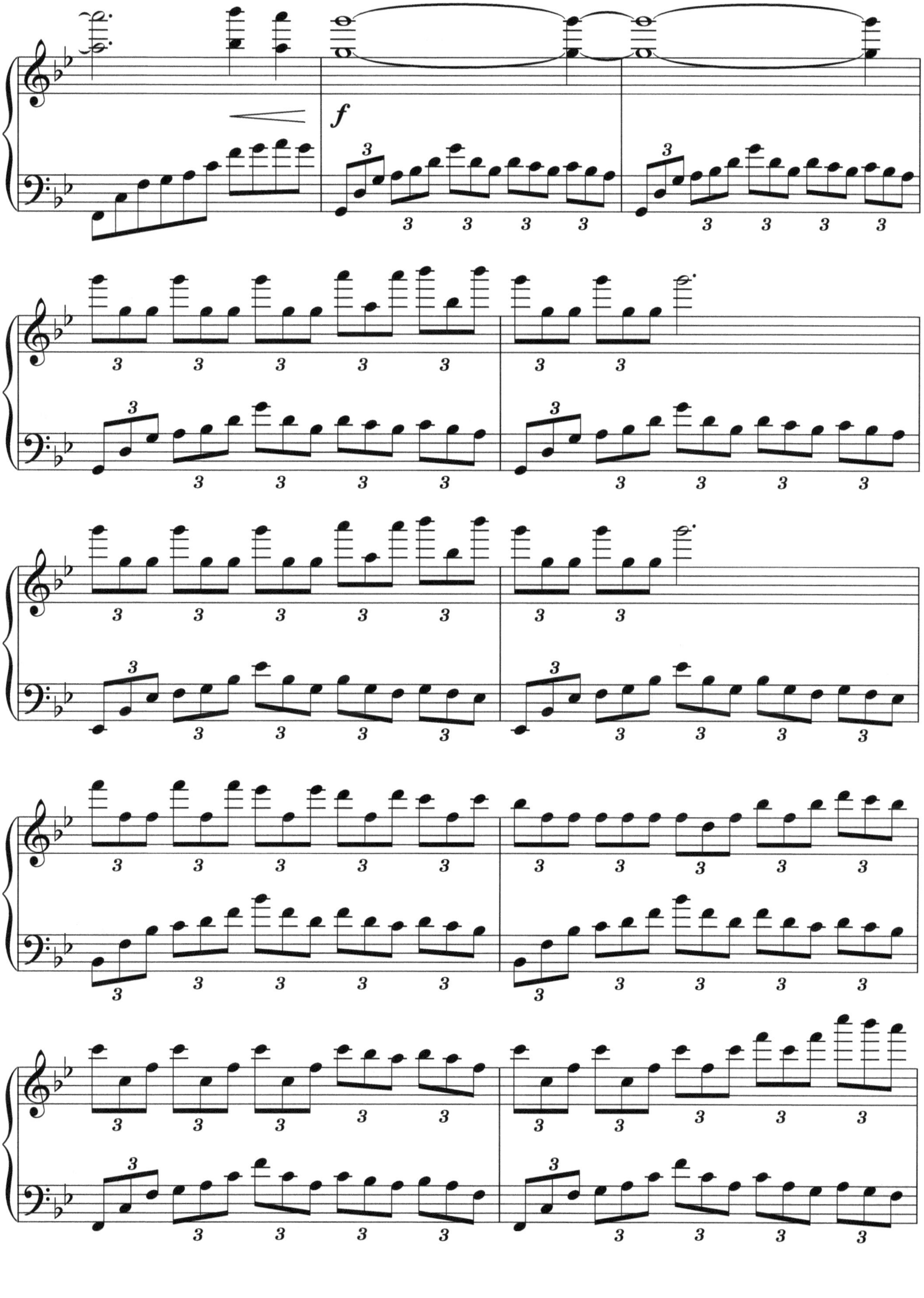
molto rit.
A tempo (♩ = 120)
f

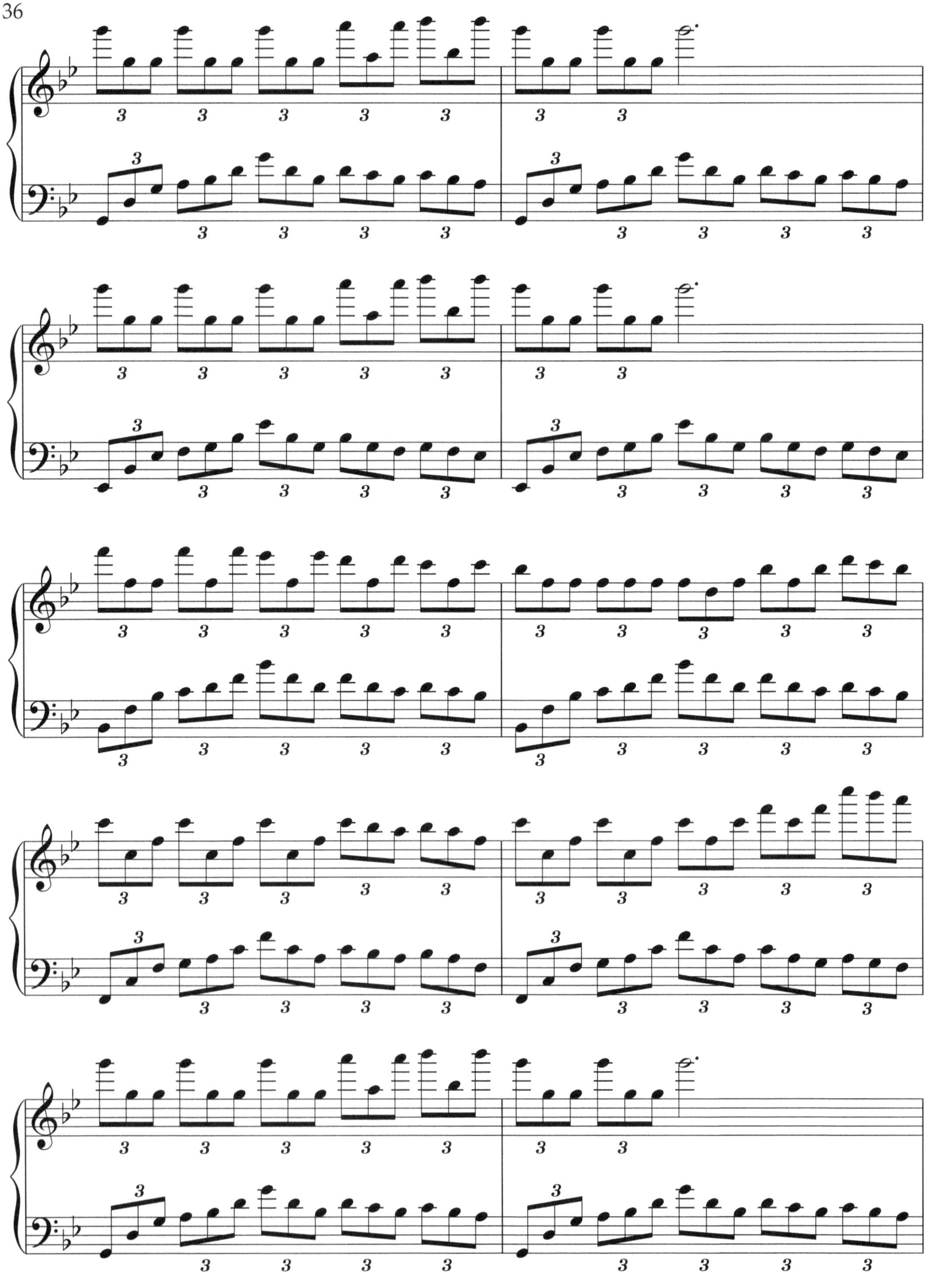

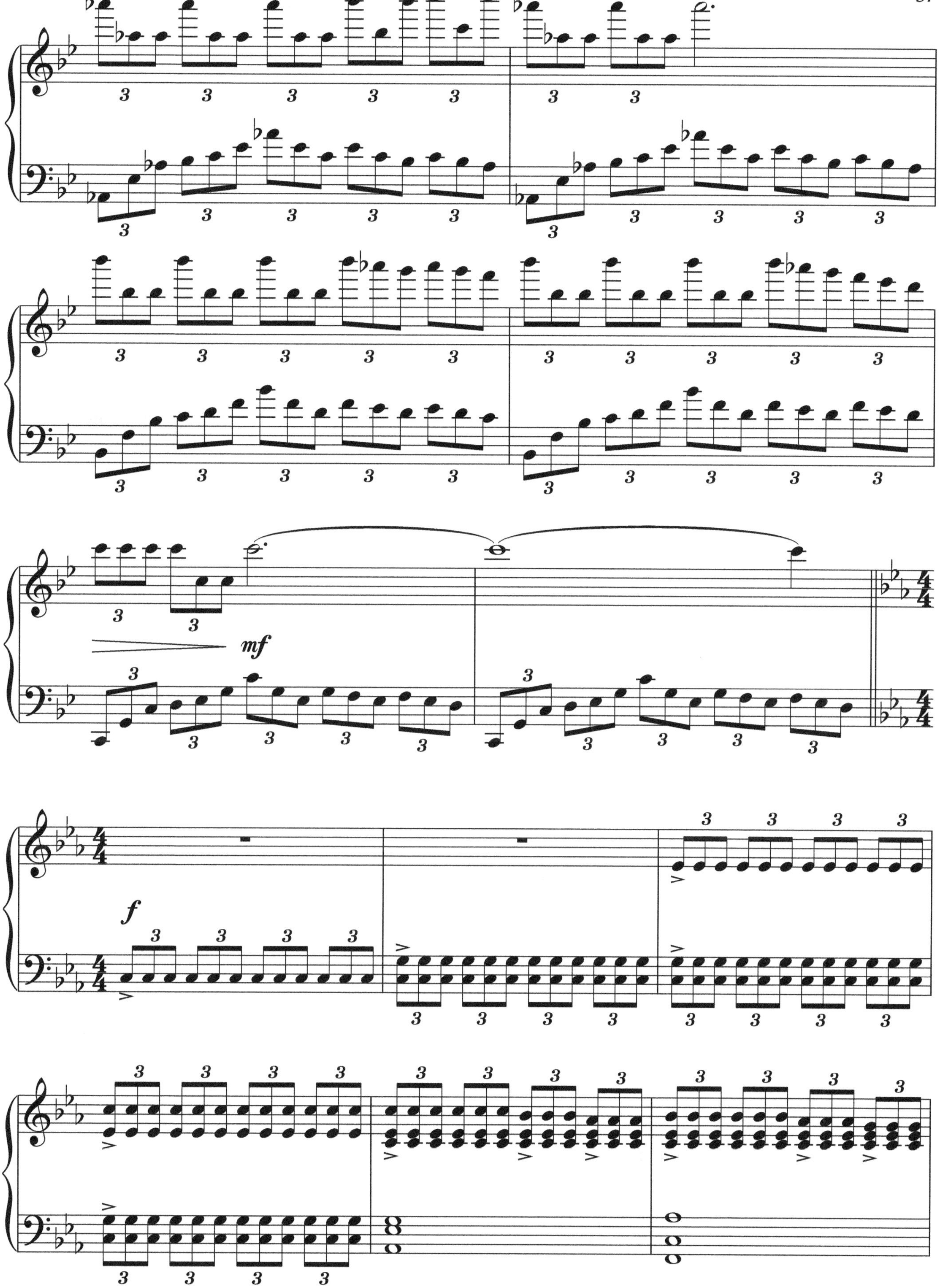
mf
f

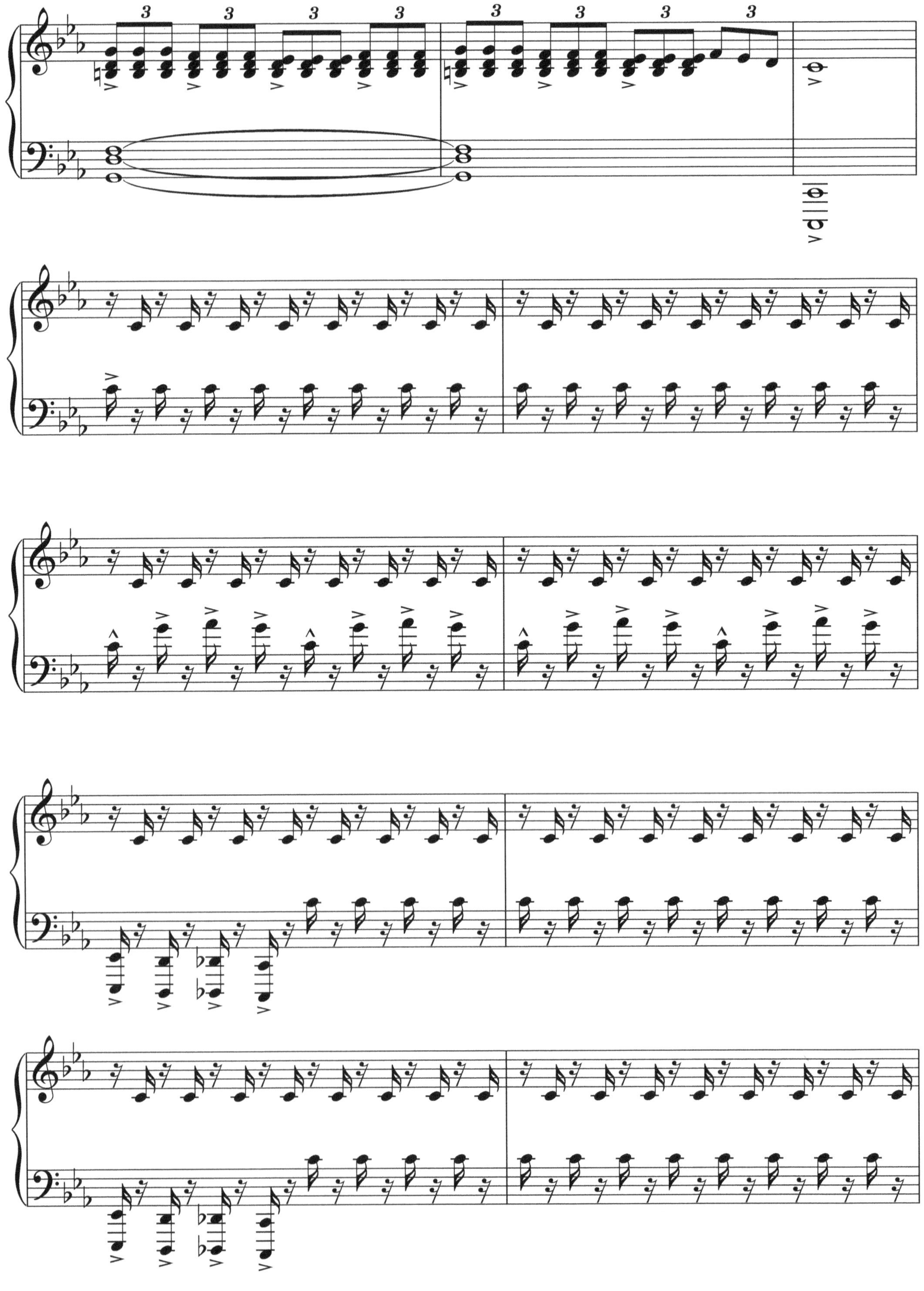
3
3
3
3
3
3
3
3

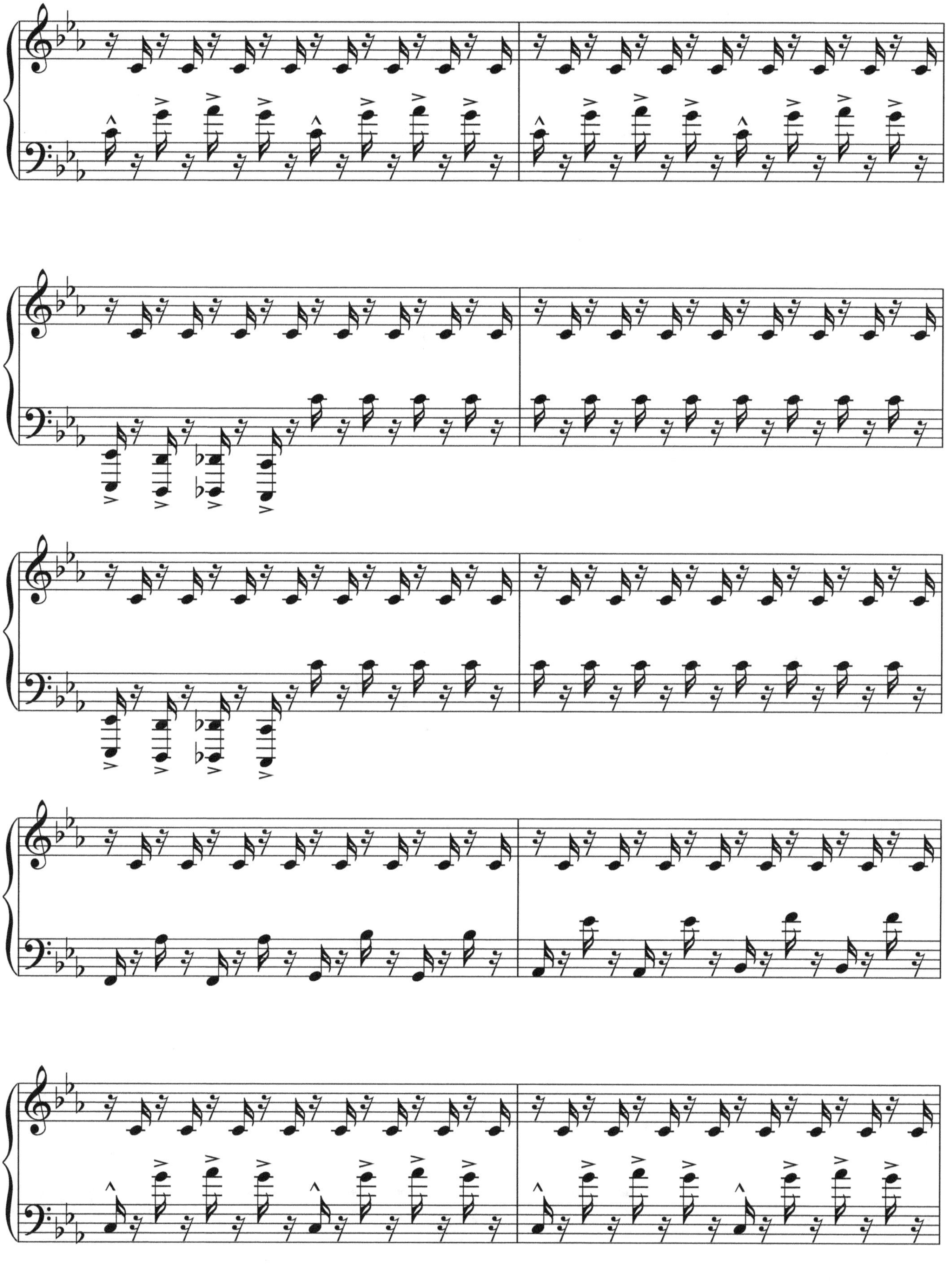

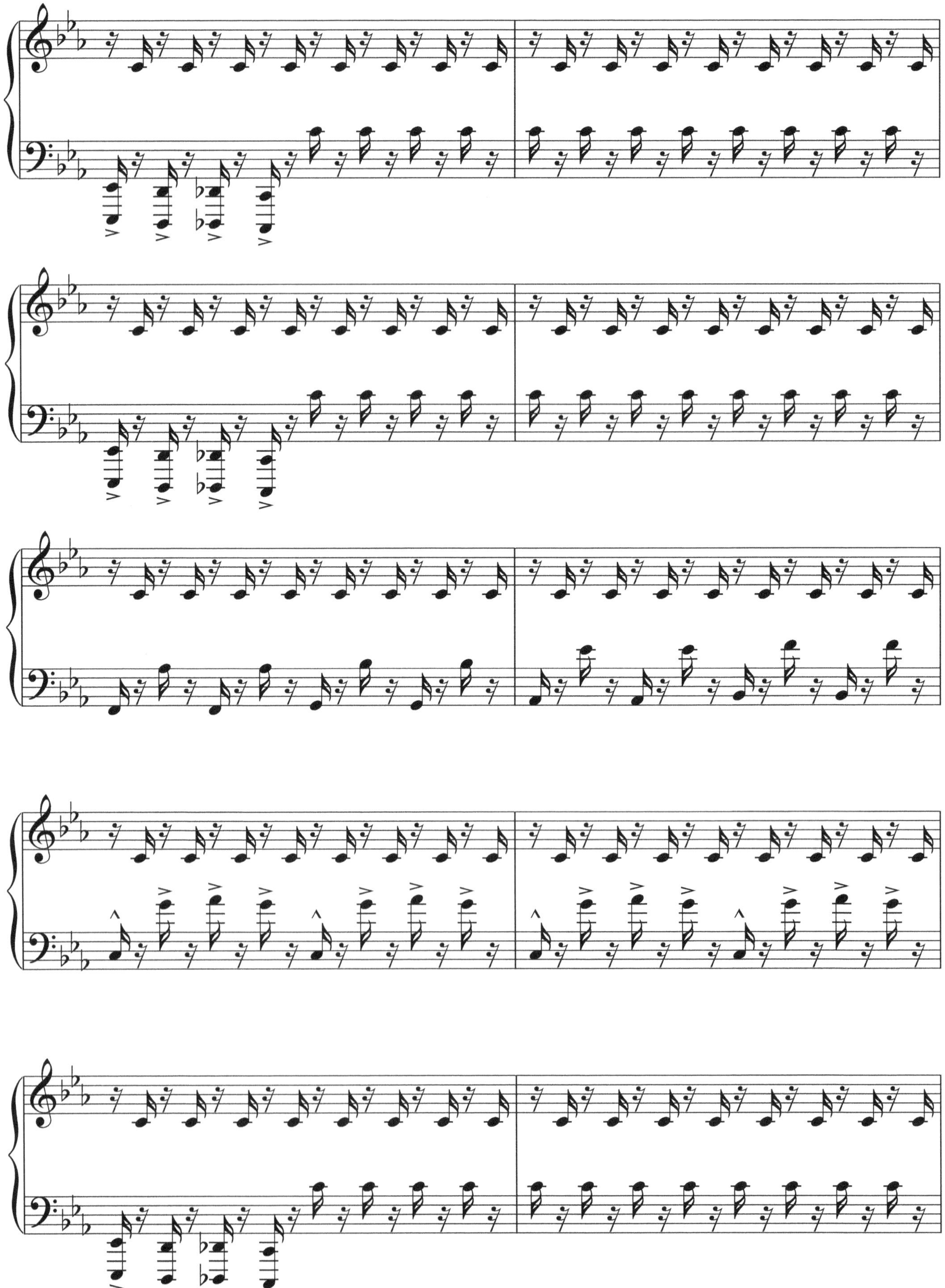

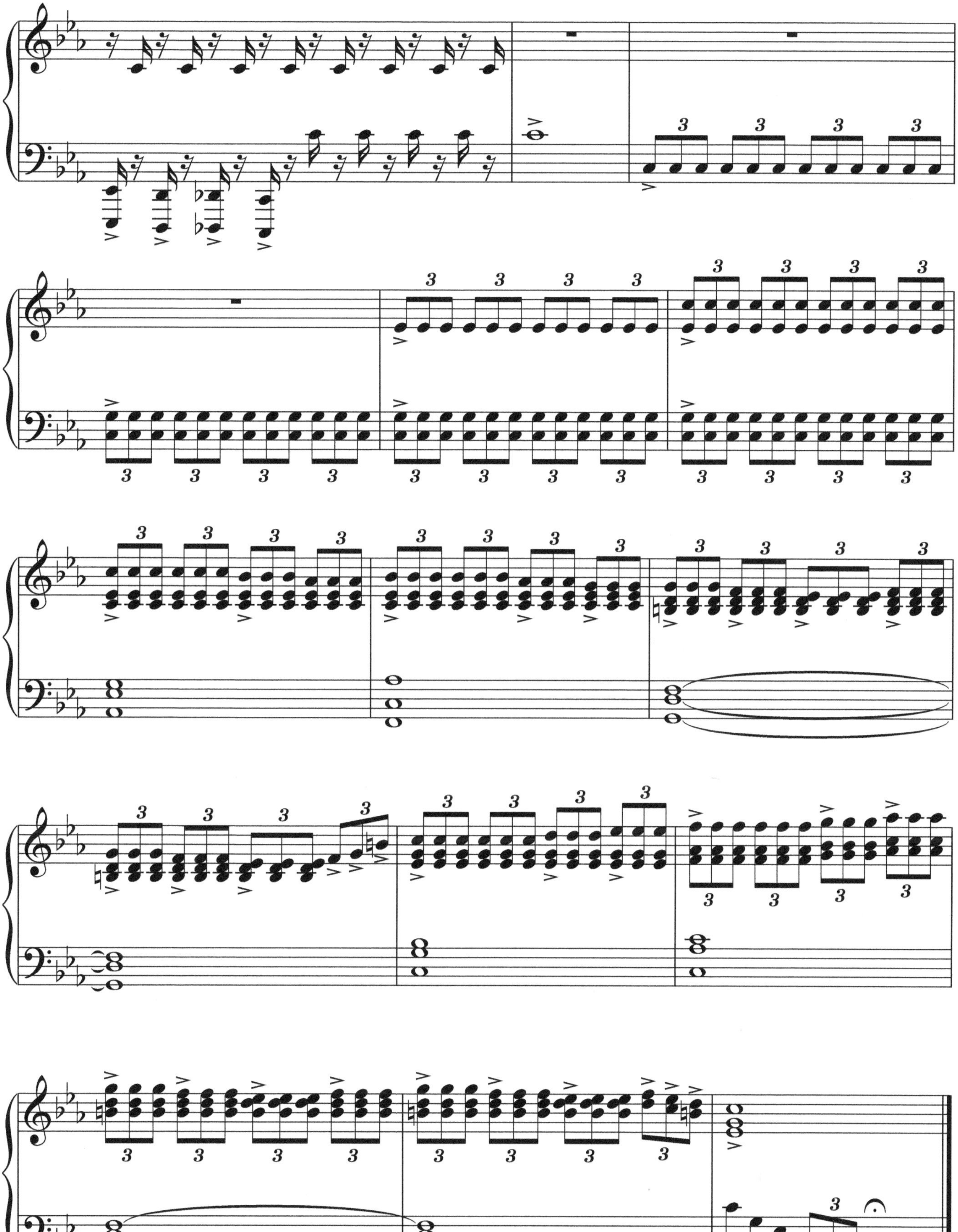
3

Into the Void

Slowly, Freely ♩ = 72

Music by Bill Walker

With pedal

accel. _ _ _ _ _ _ _ _ _ _ _ _ _ _

grad. cresc. and descres. throughout the entire piece

Hypnotically ♩ = 160

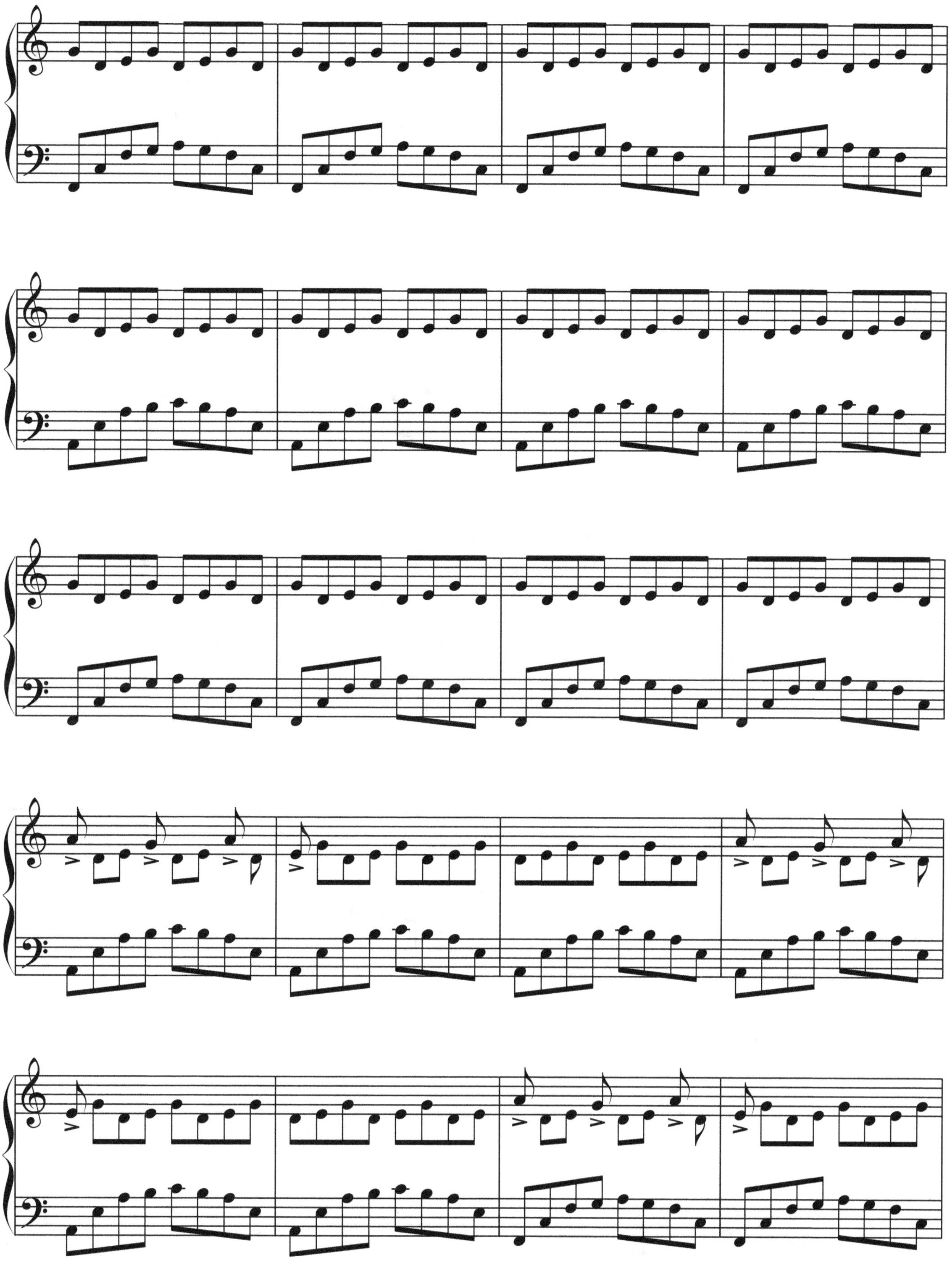

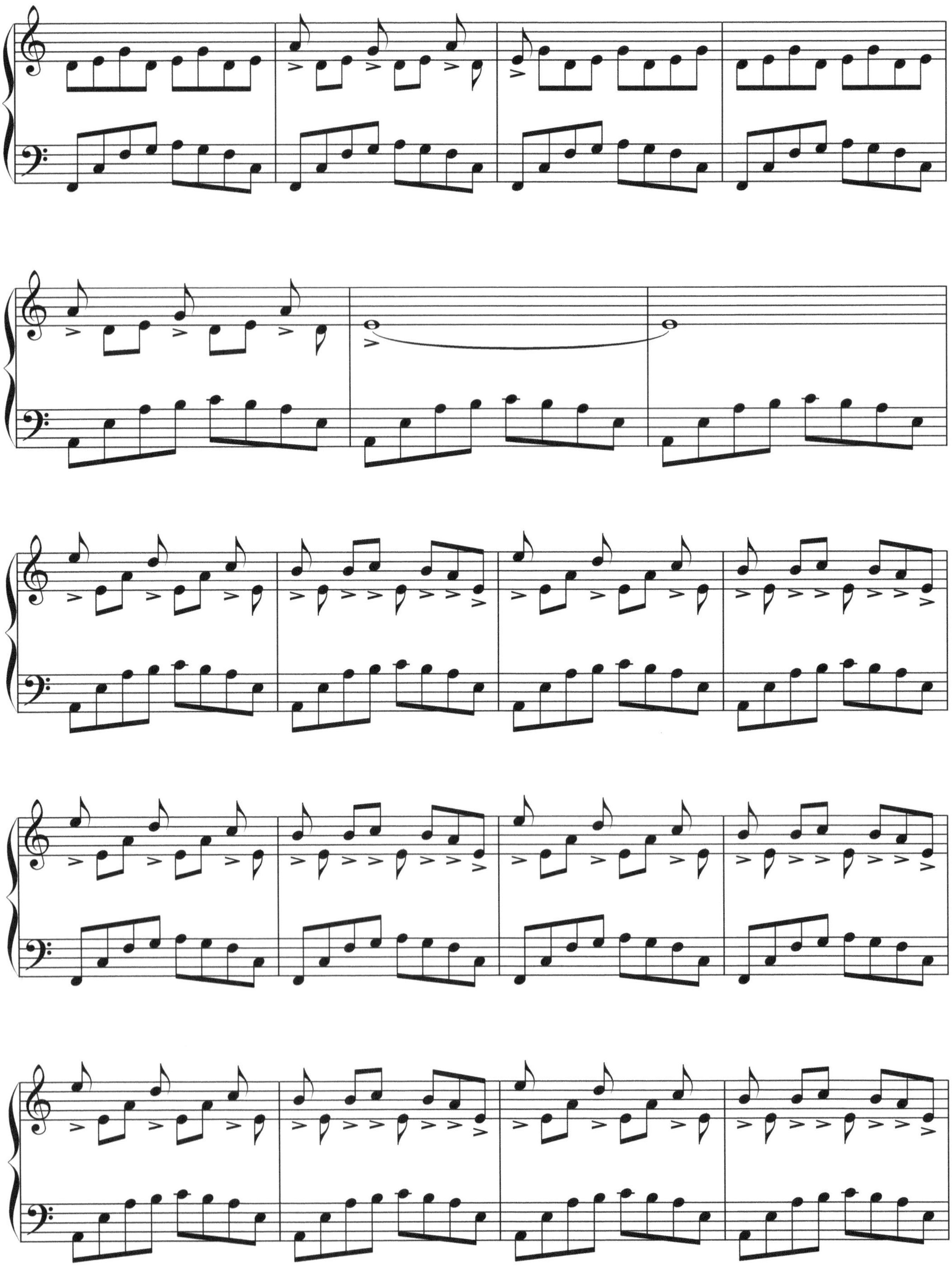

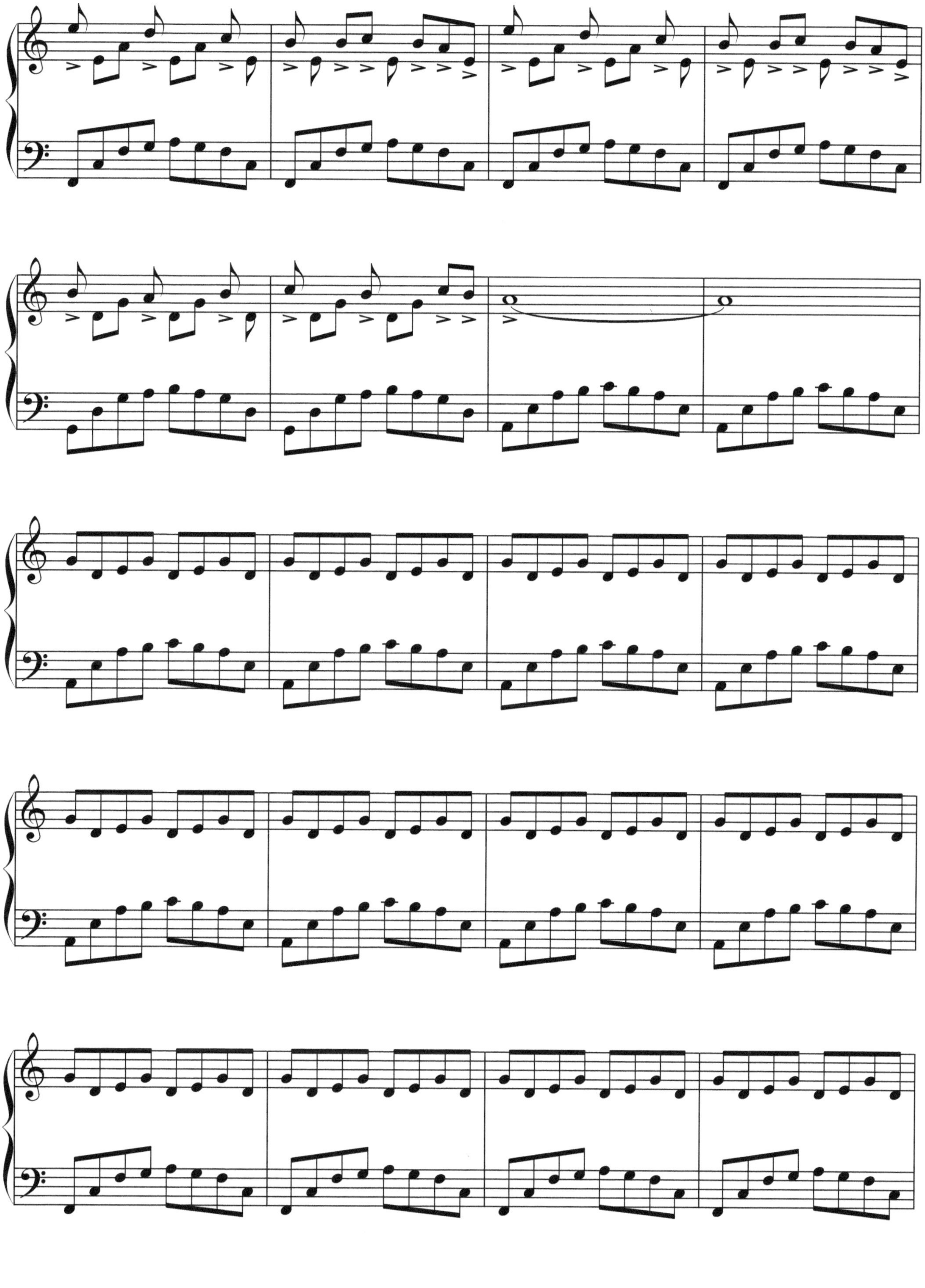

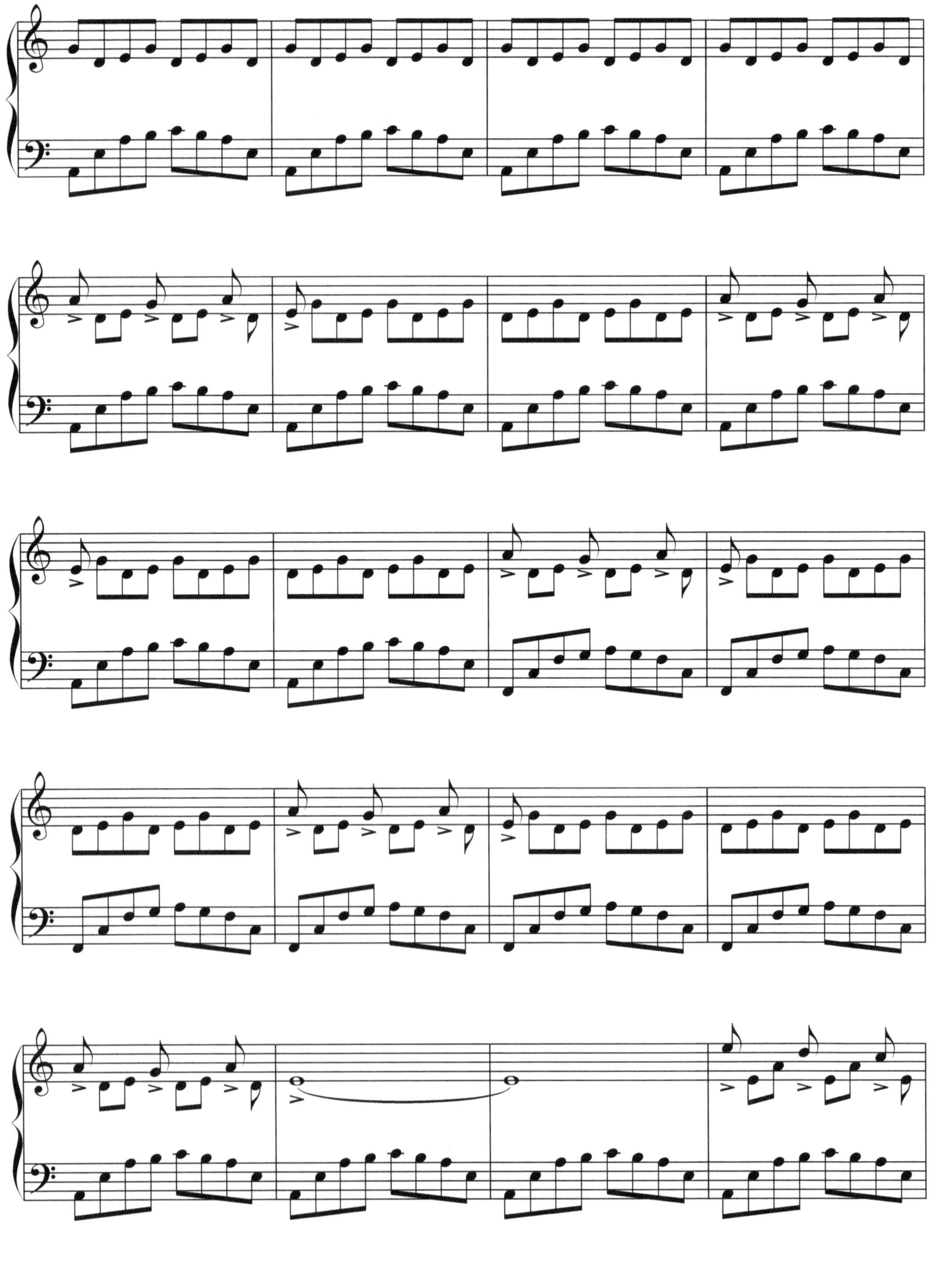

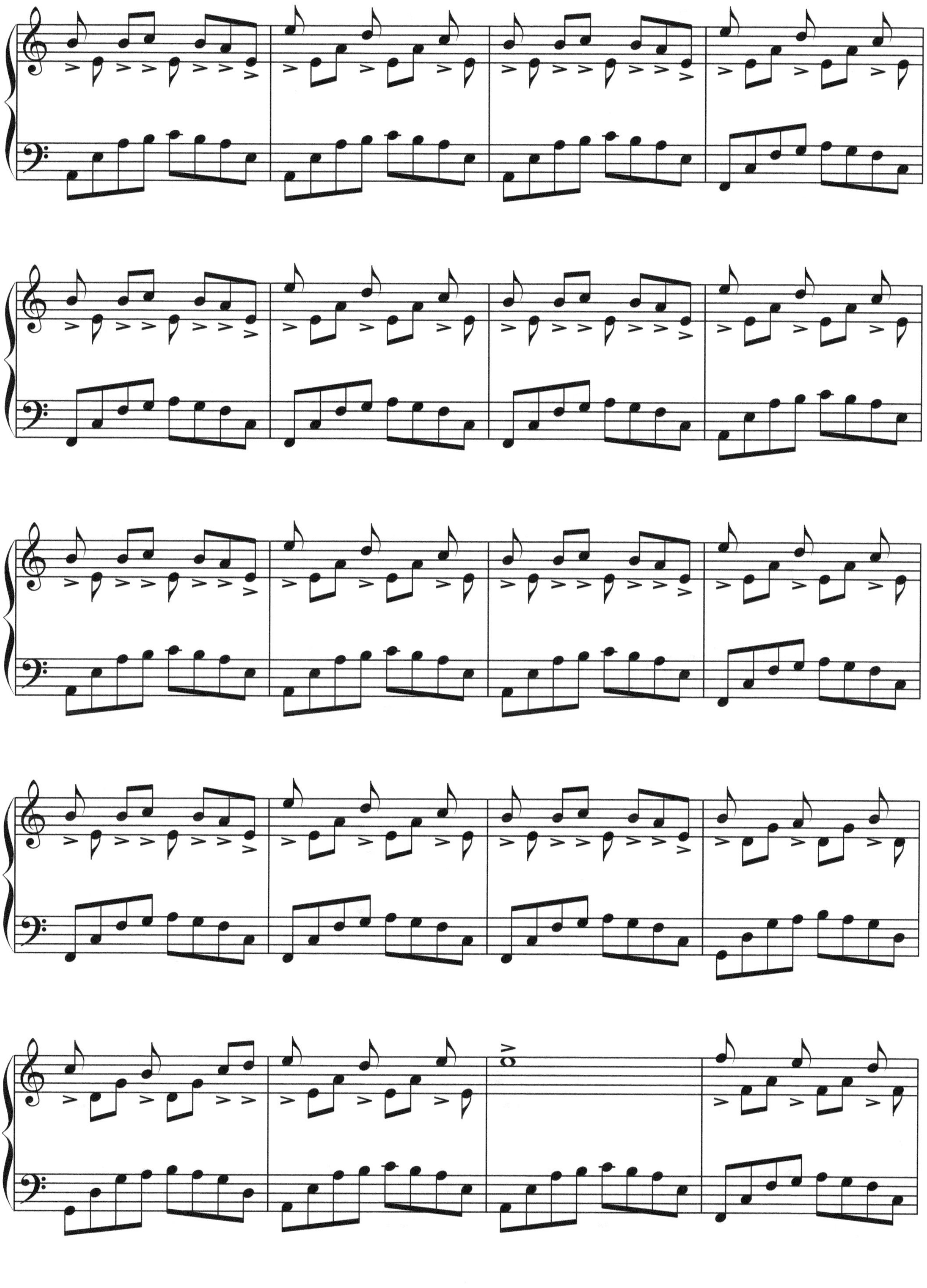

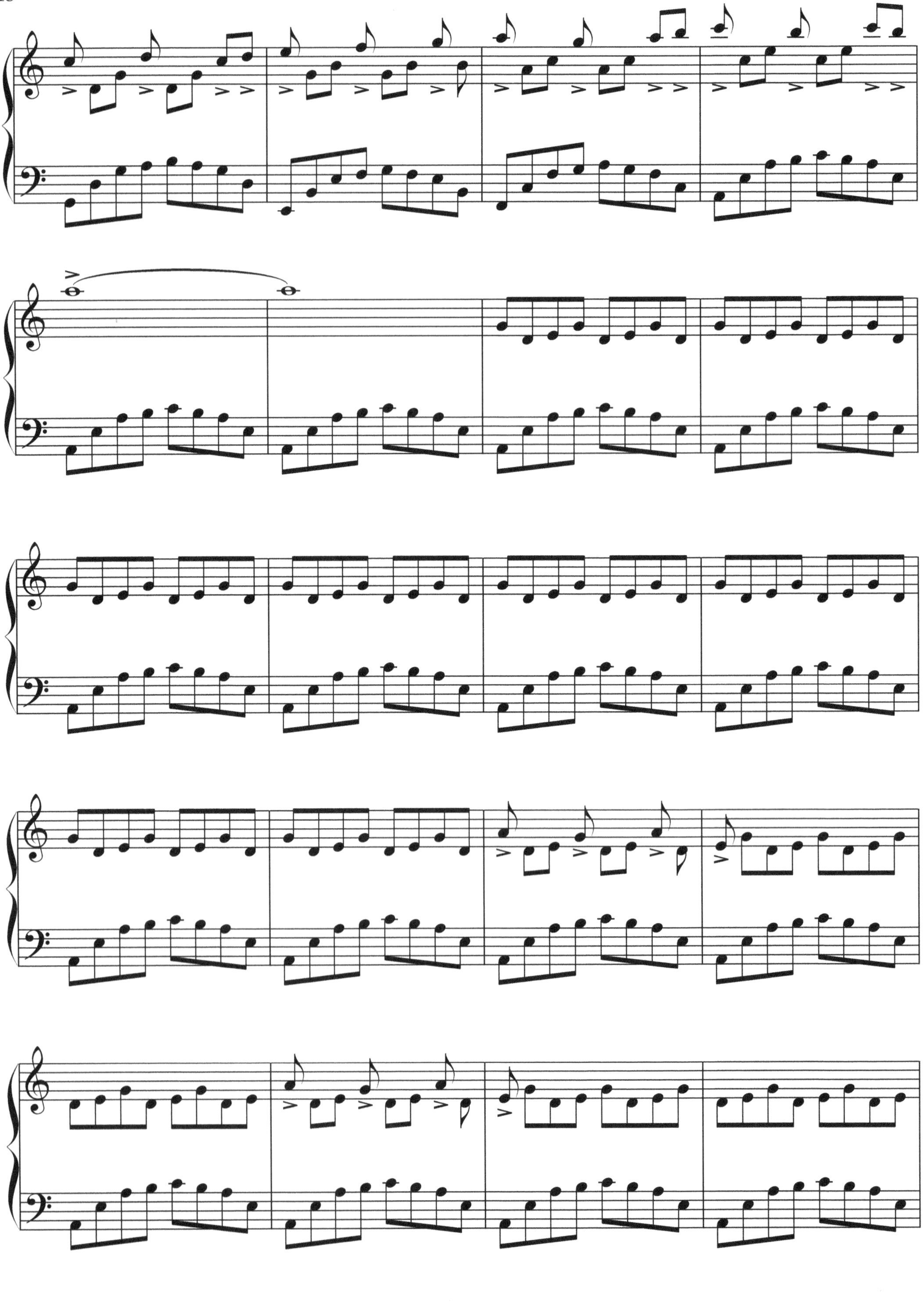

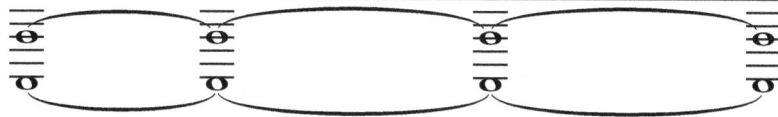

Final Rites

Music by Bill Walker

Allegro (♩ = 136)

With pedal

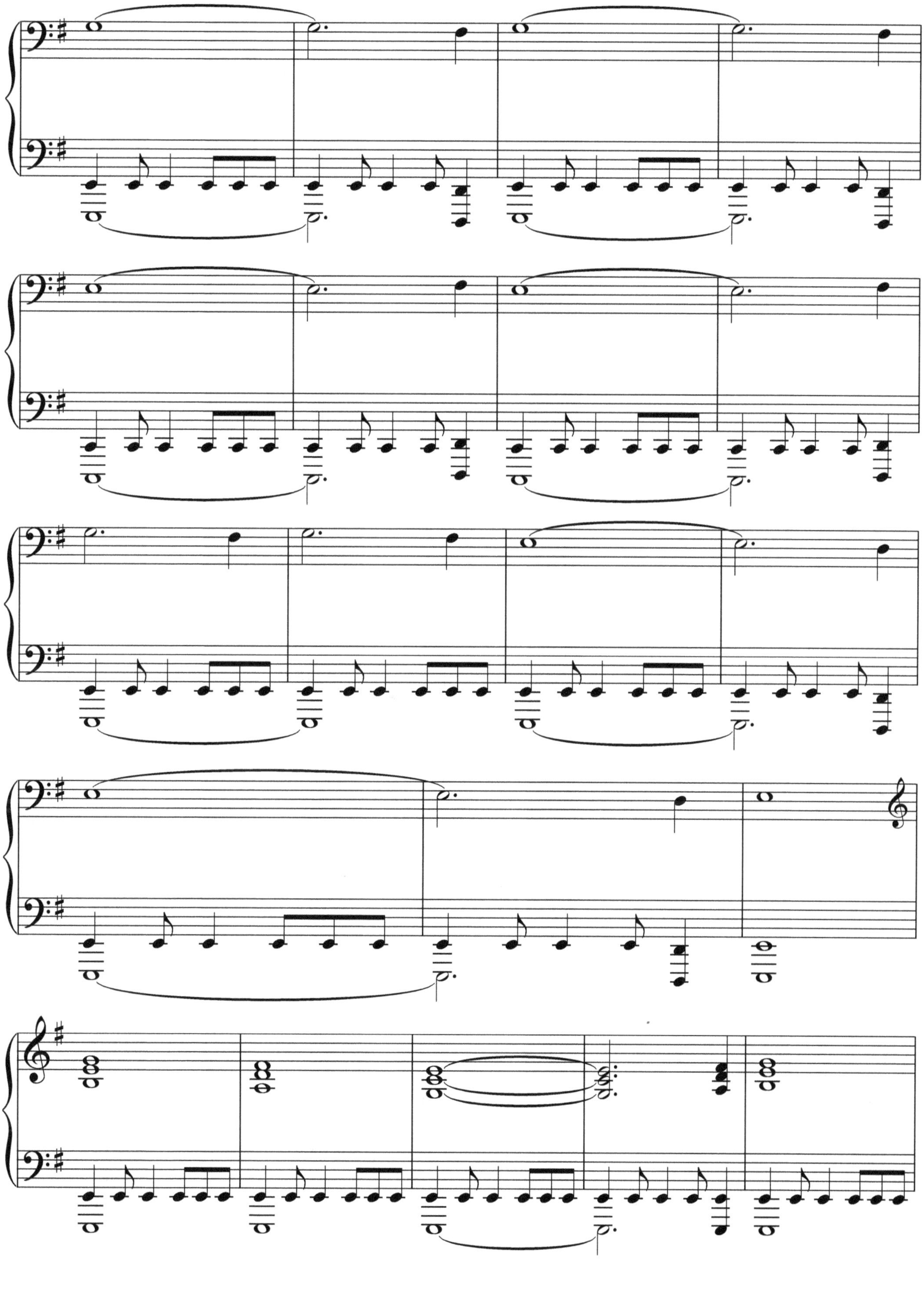

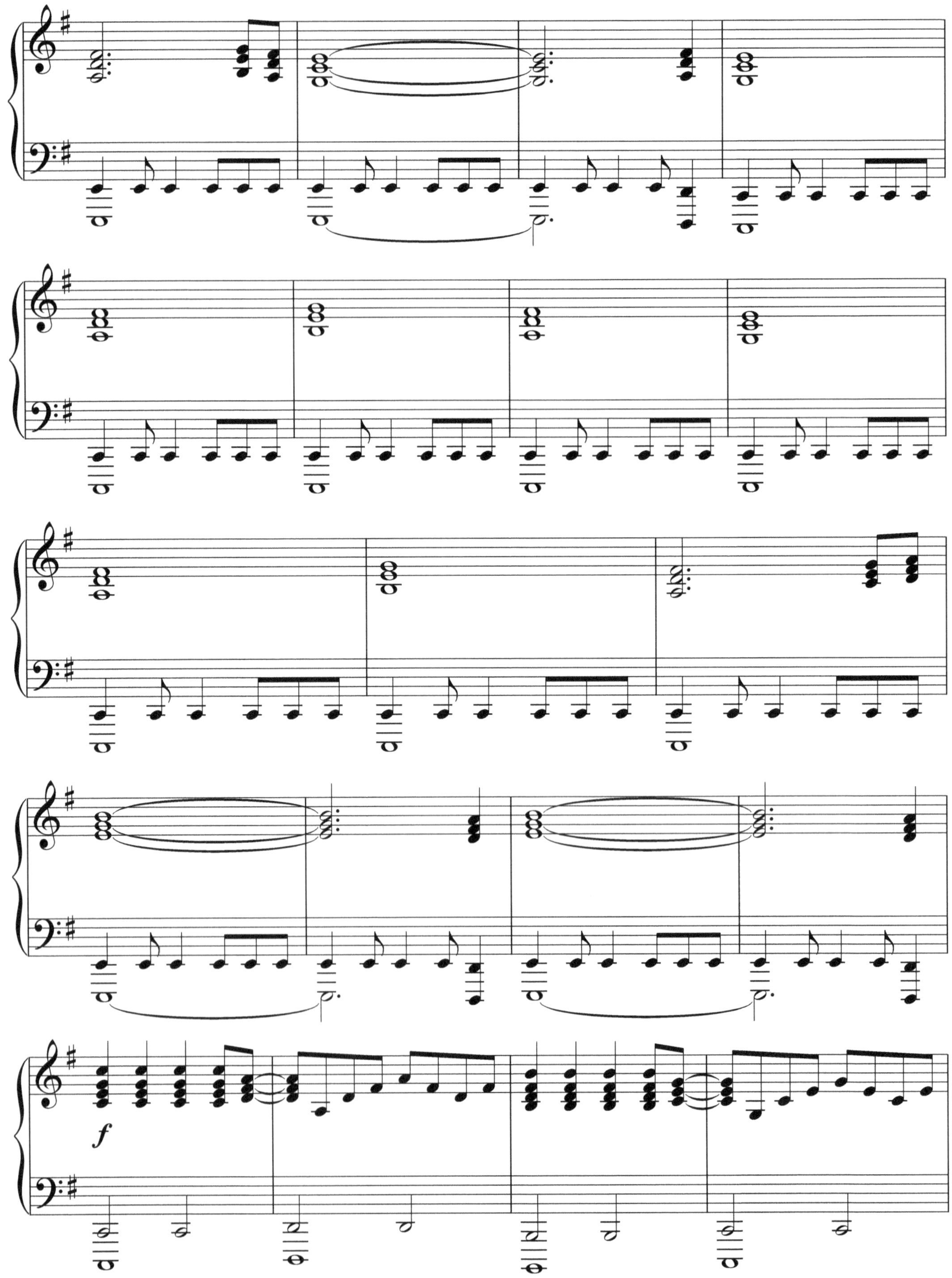
f

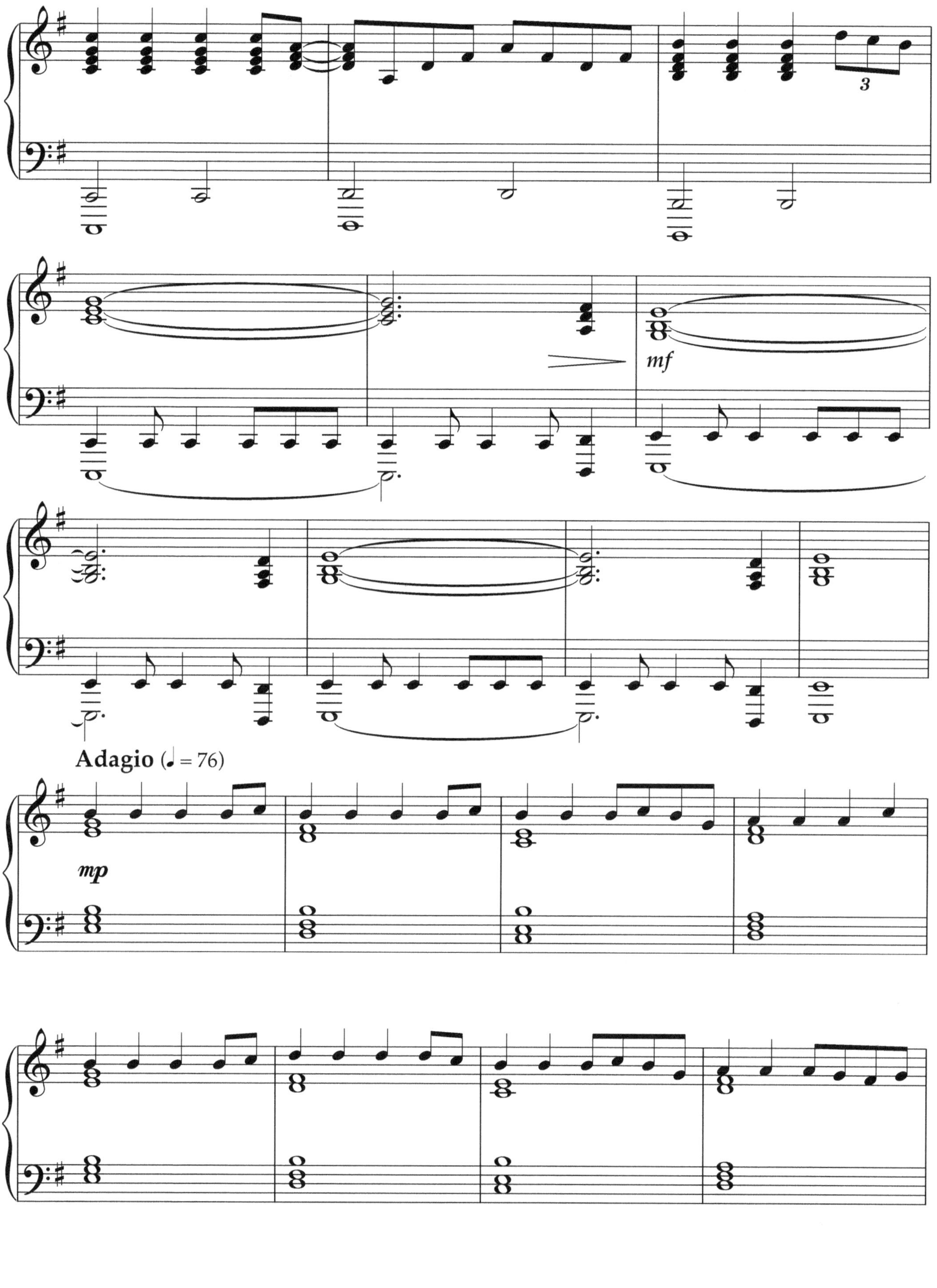
3
mf
Adagio (♩ = 76)
mp

Tempo primo (♩ = 136)

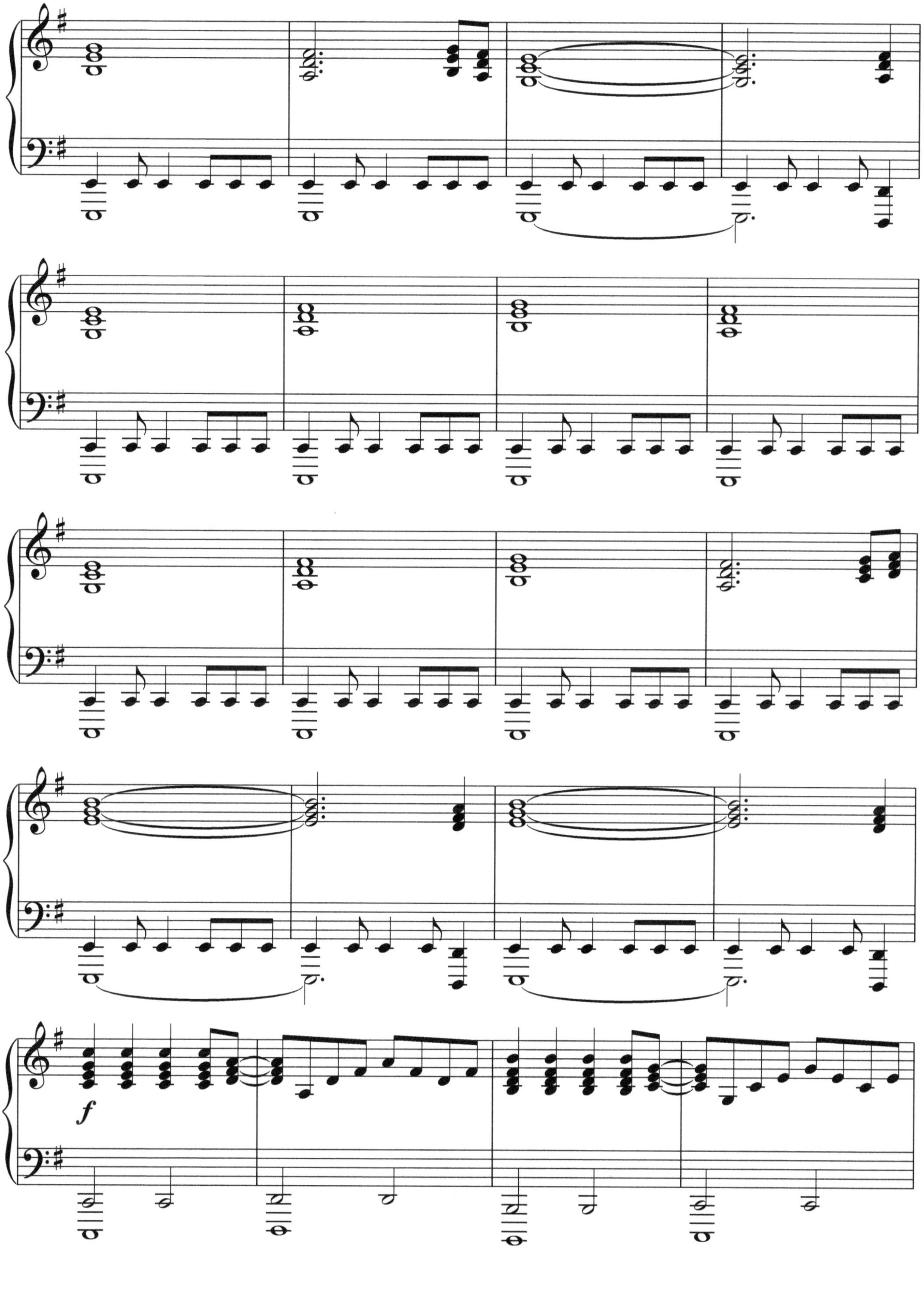
f

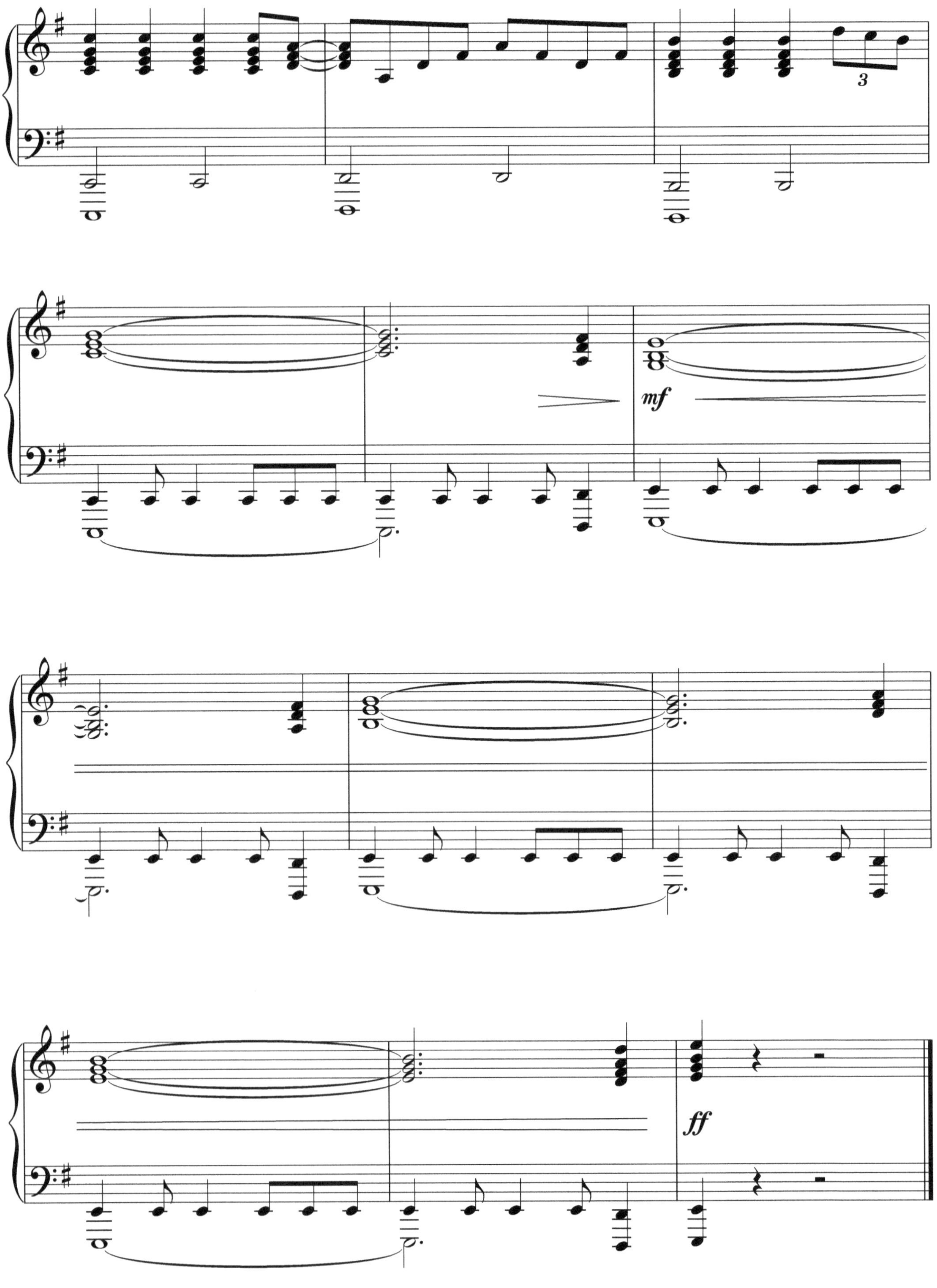
3
mf
ff

Threads of Time

Music by Bill Walker

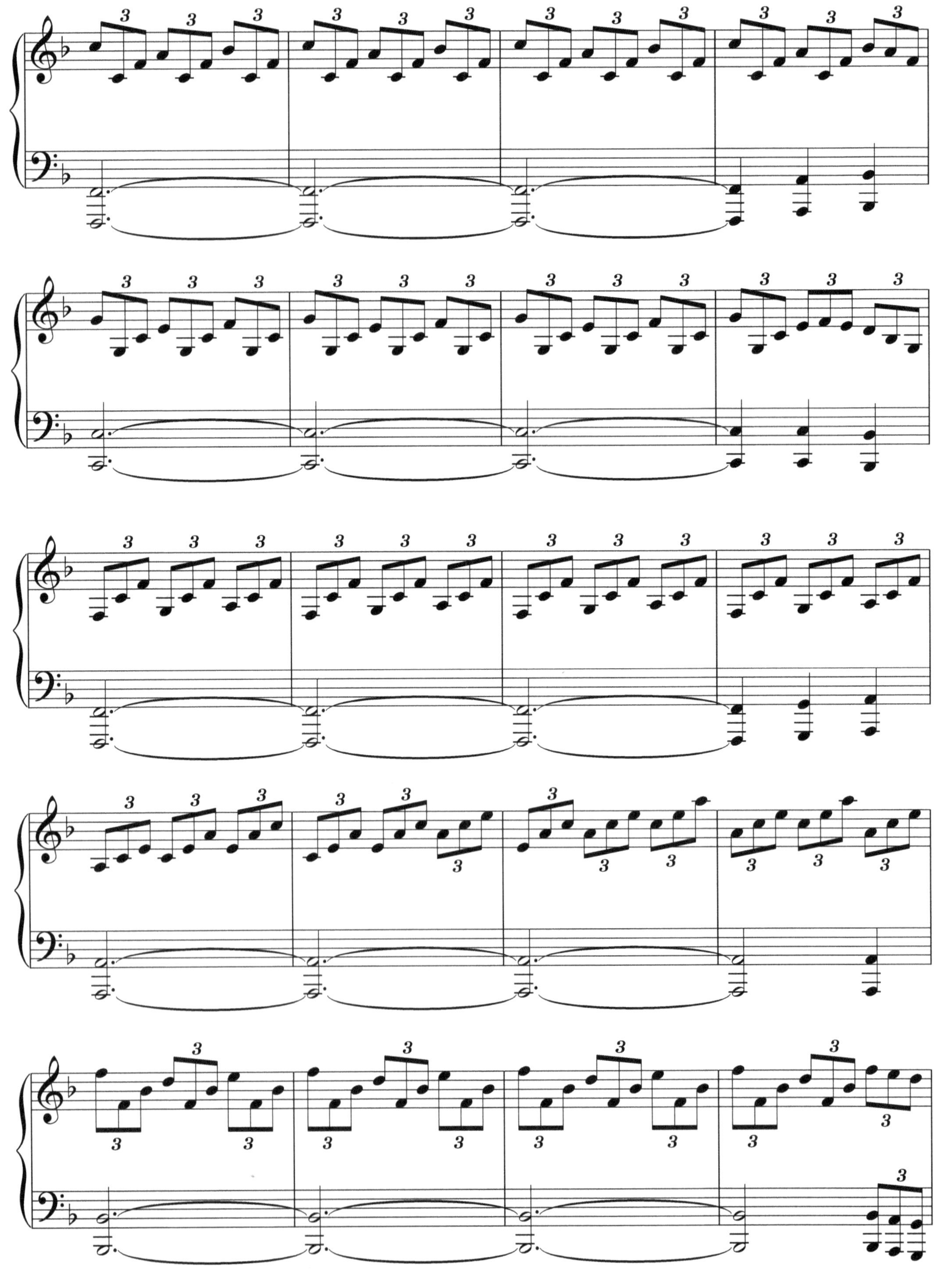
3
3
3

molto rit.

With sad determination (♩ = 104)

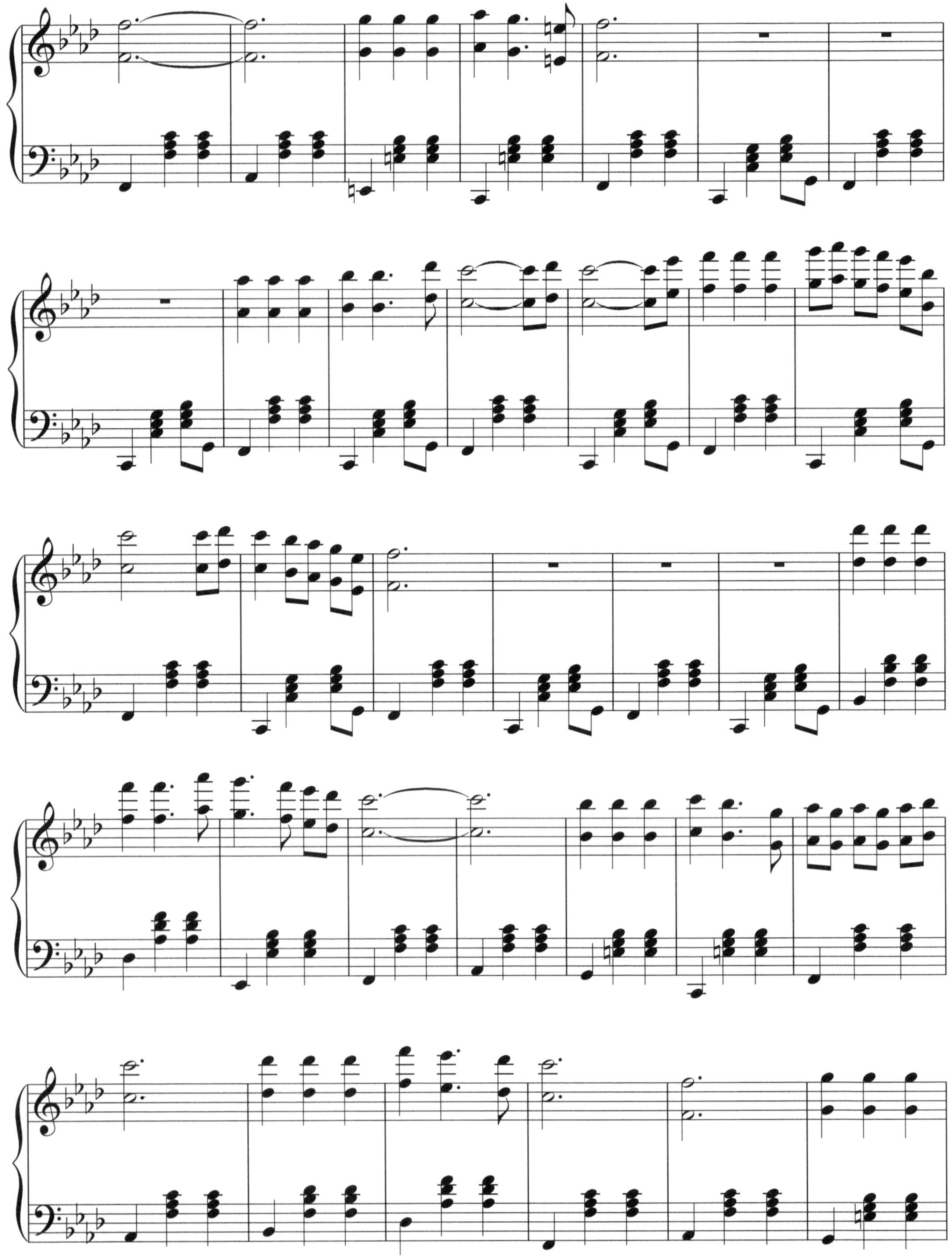

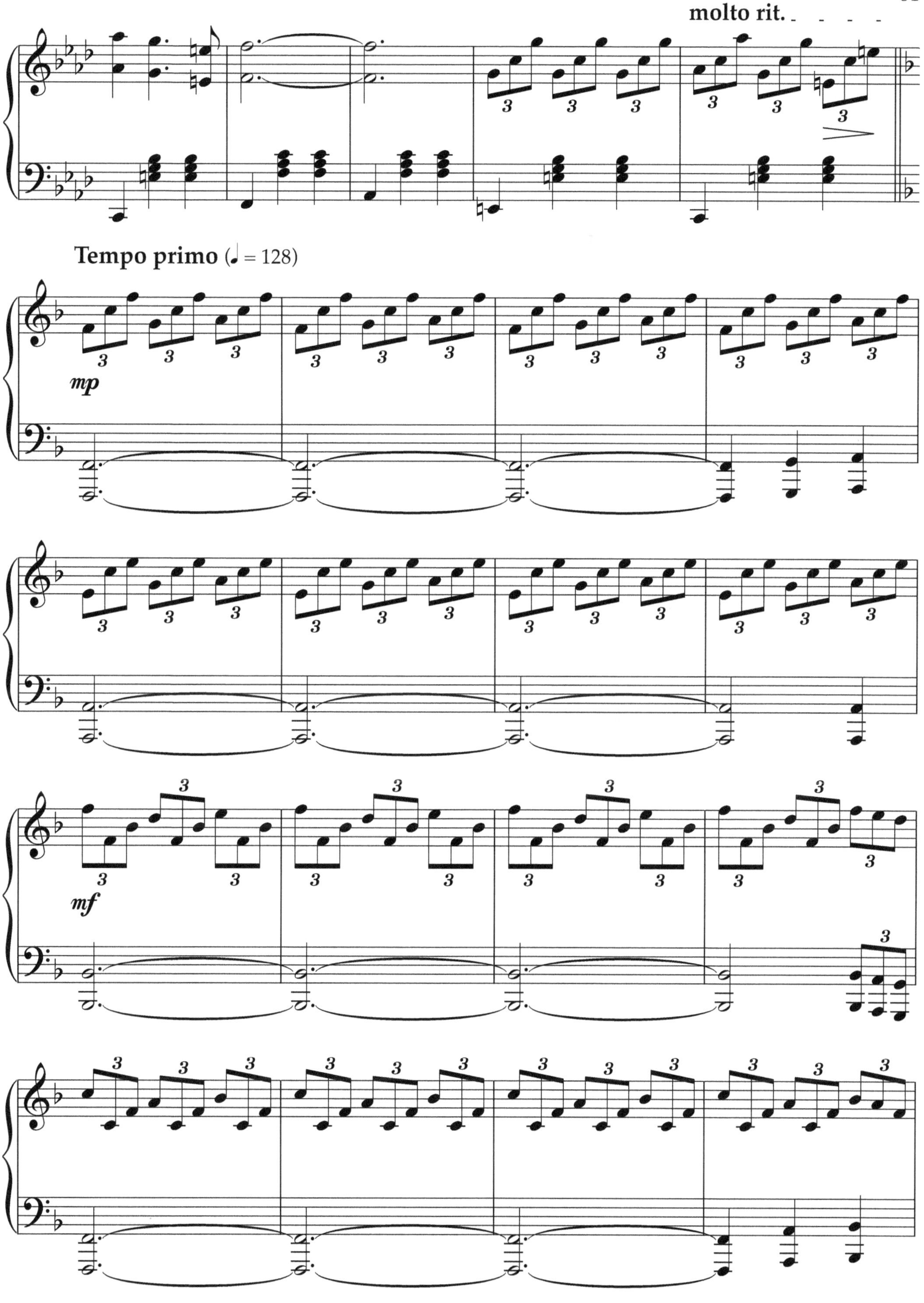
molto rit.
Tempo primo (♩ = 128)
mp
mf

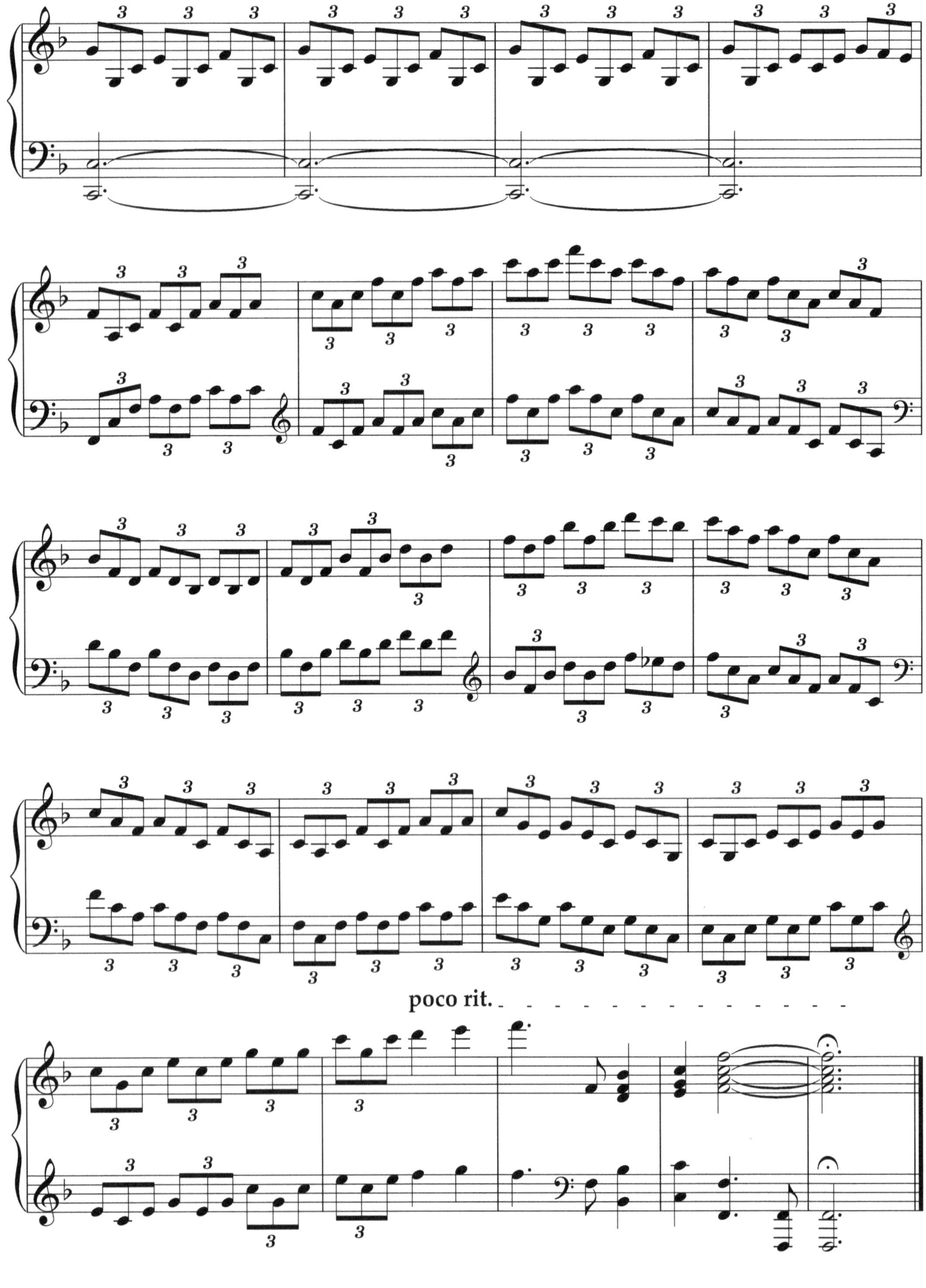
poco rit.

The Light Through the Shadows

Music by Bill Walker

Allegro (♩ = 140)

With pedal

(R.H.)

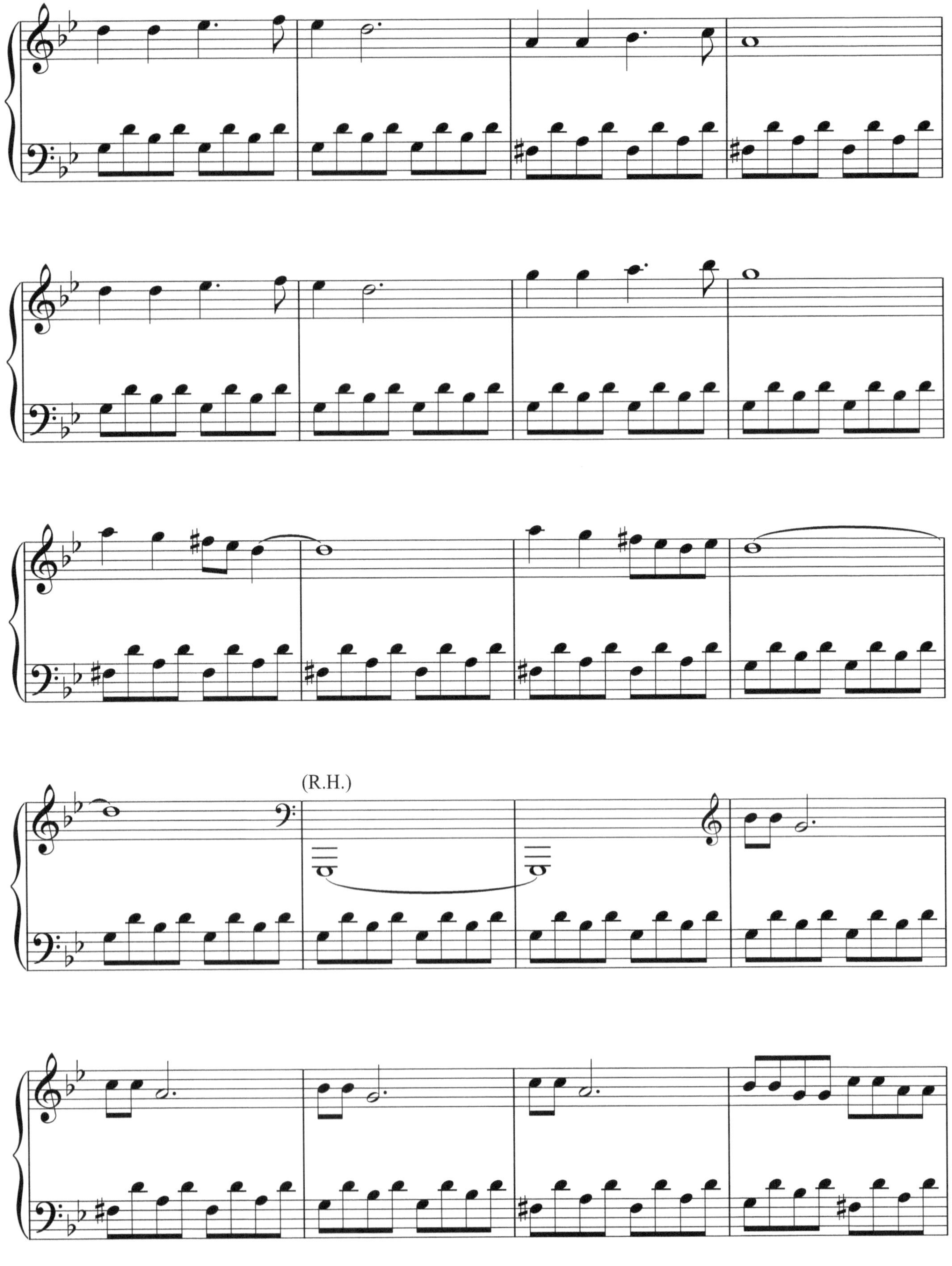
(R.H.)

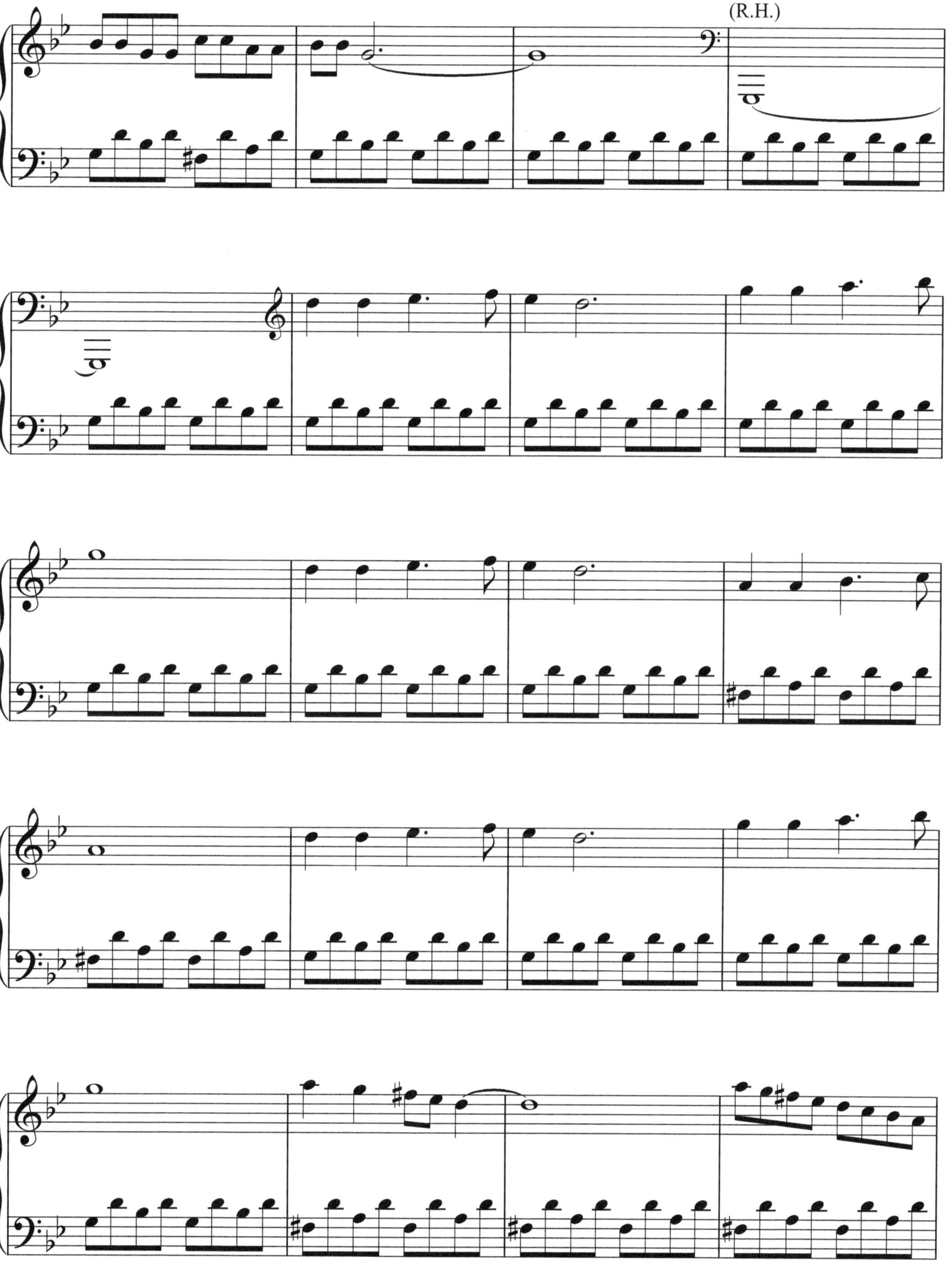
(R.H.)

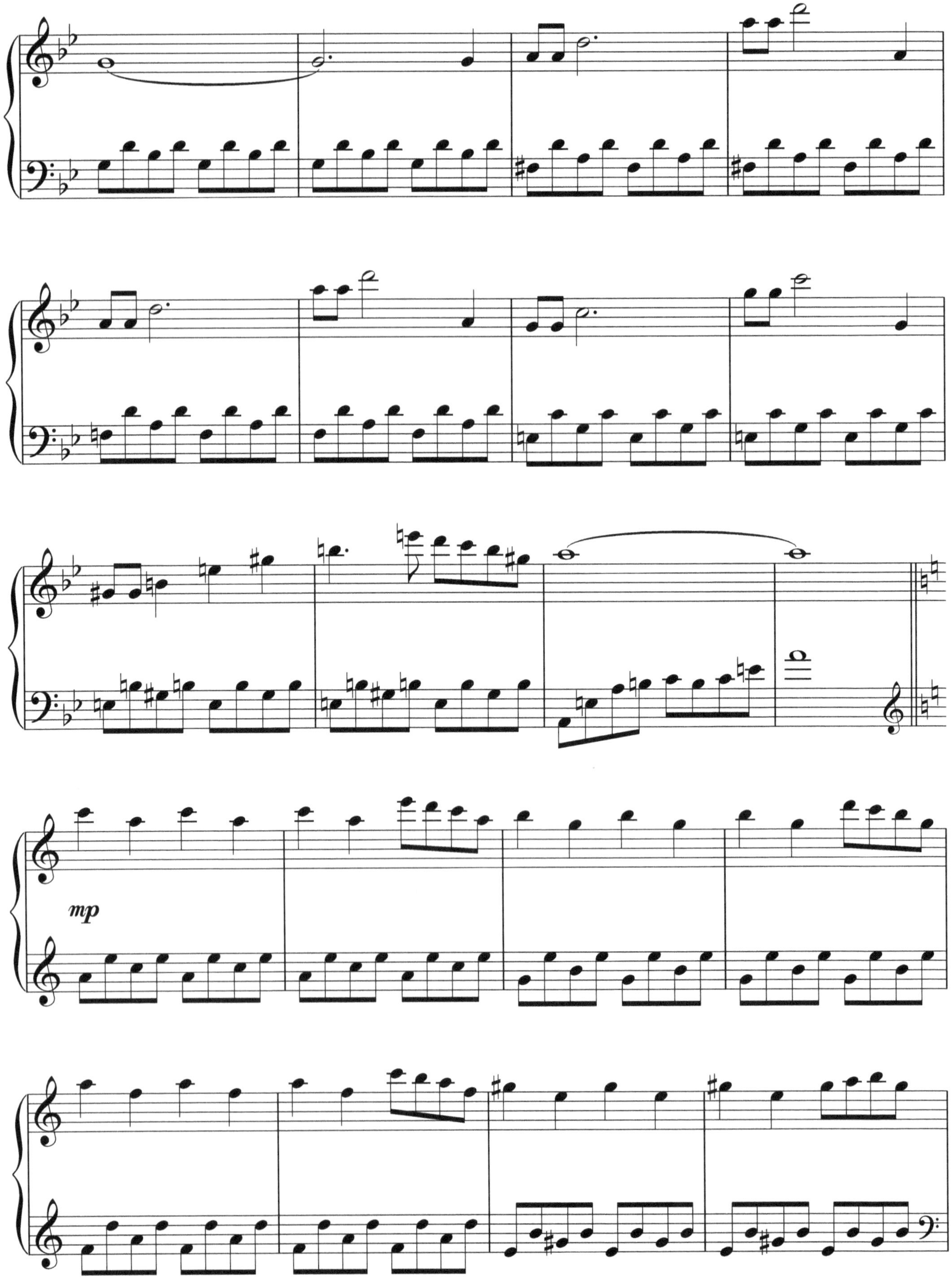
mp

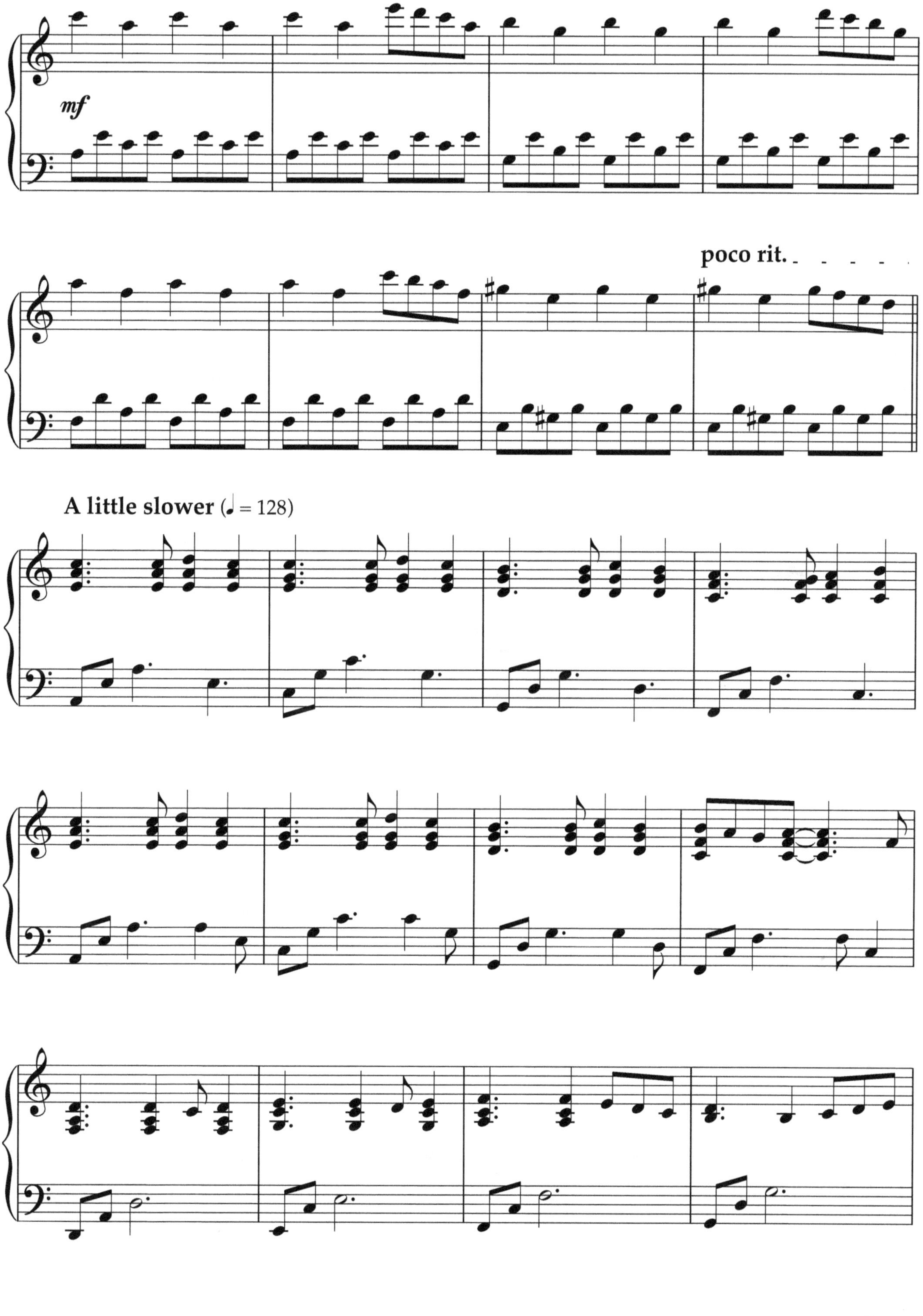
mf
poco rit.
A little slower (♩. = 128)

Tempo primo (♩ = 140)

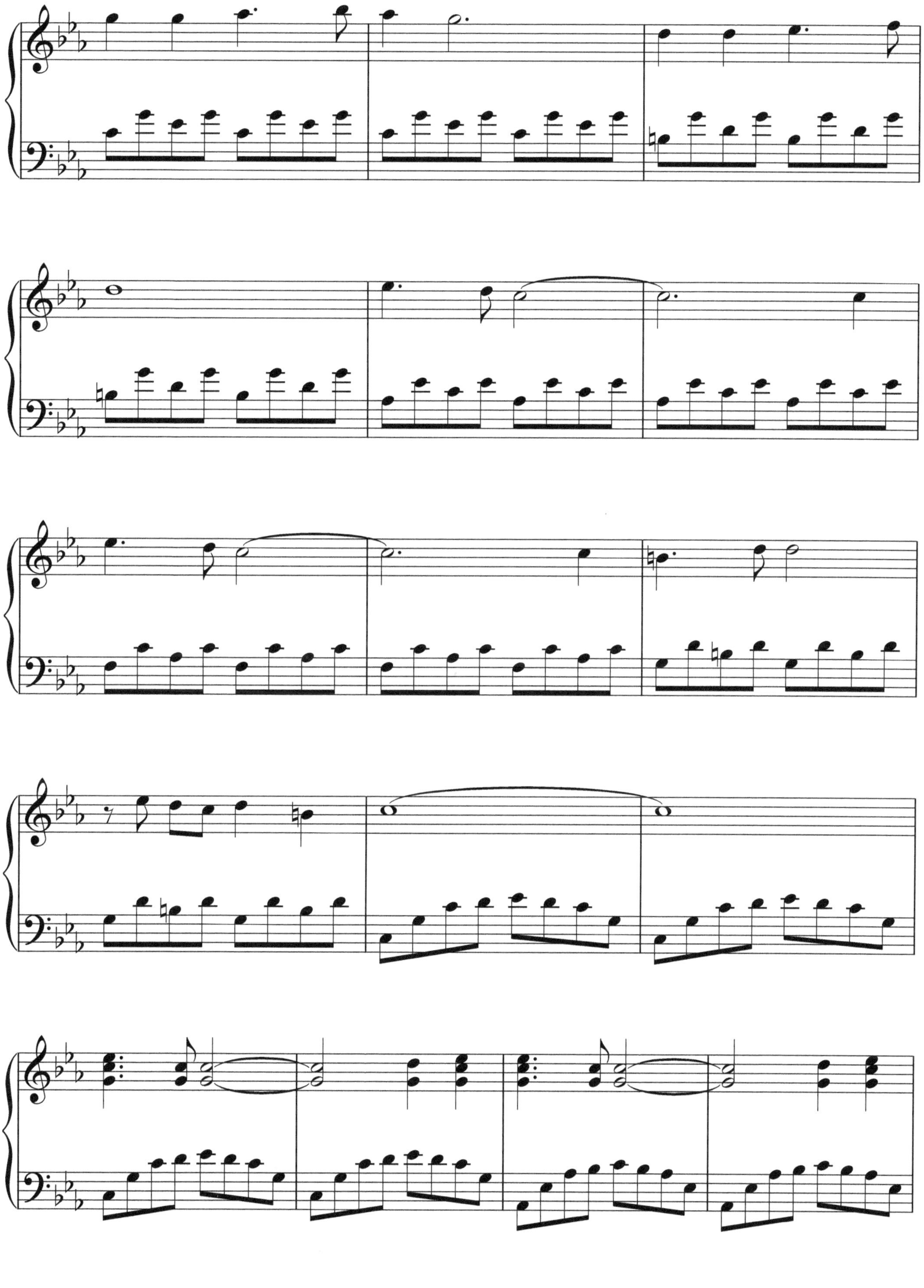

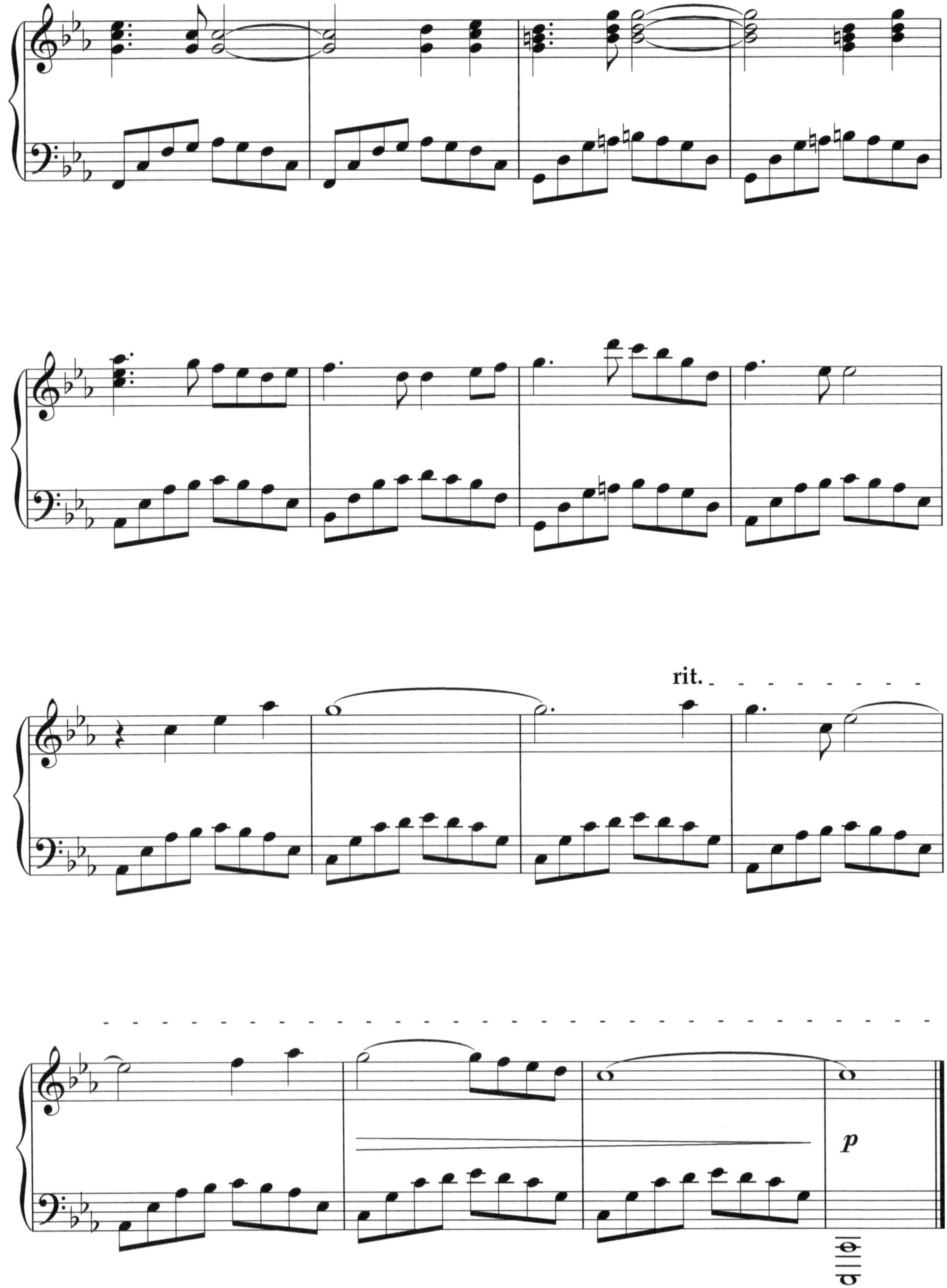
rit.
p

Serenity's Storm

Music by Bill Walker

Thoughtfully ($\quarternote = 100$)

With pedal

rit.

Pulsating, Forward Motion ($\quarternote = 124$)

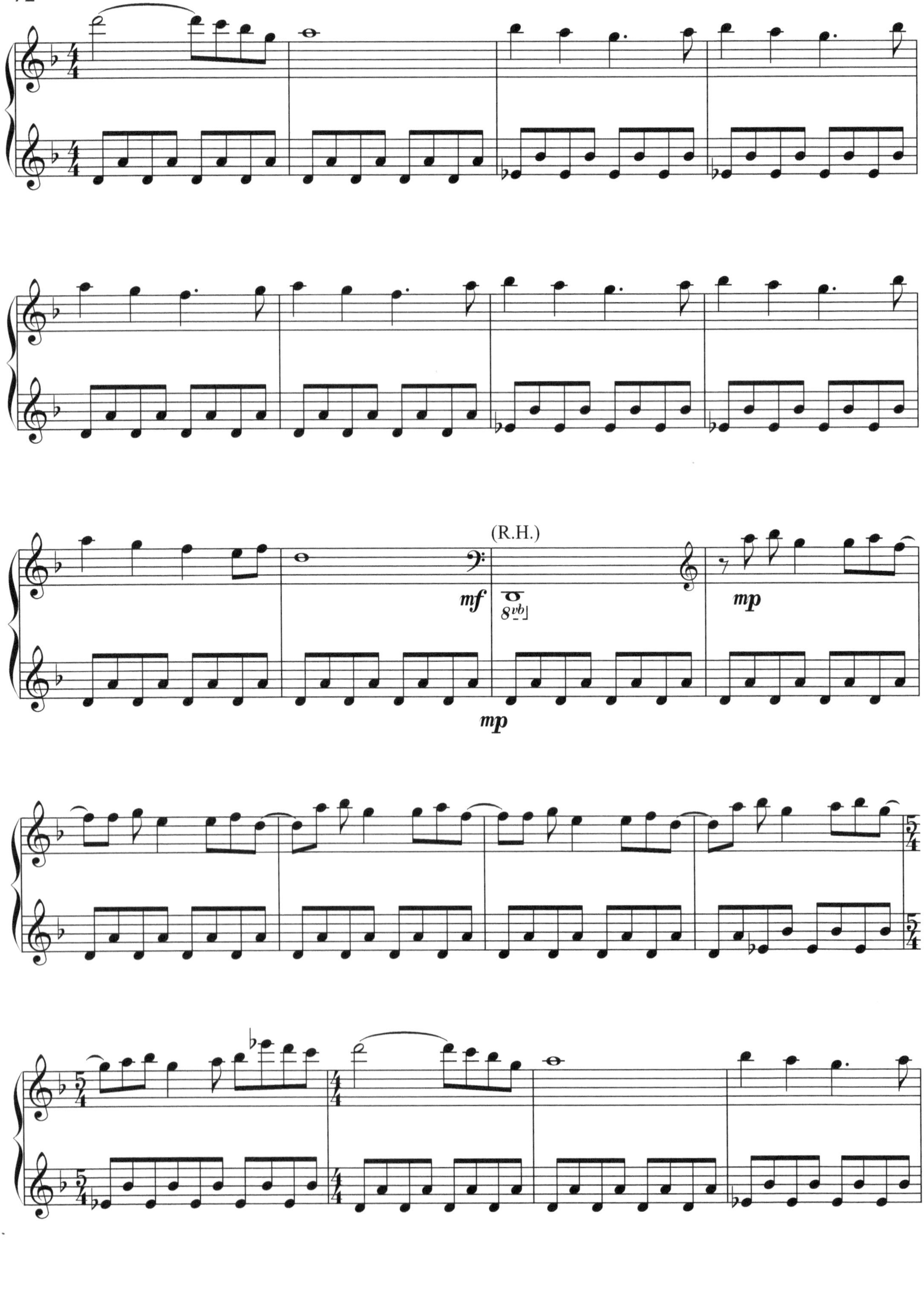
(R.H.)
mf
8vb
mp
mp
mp

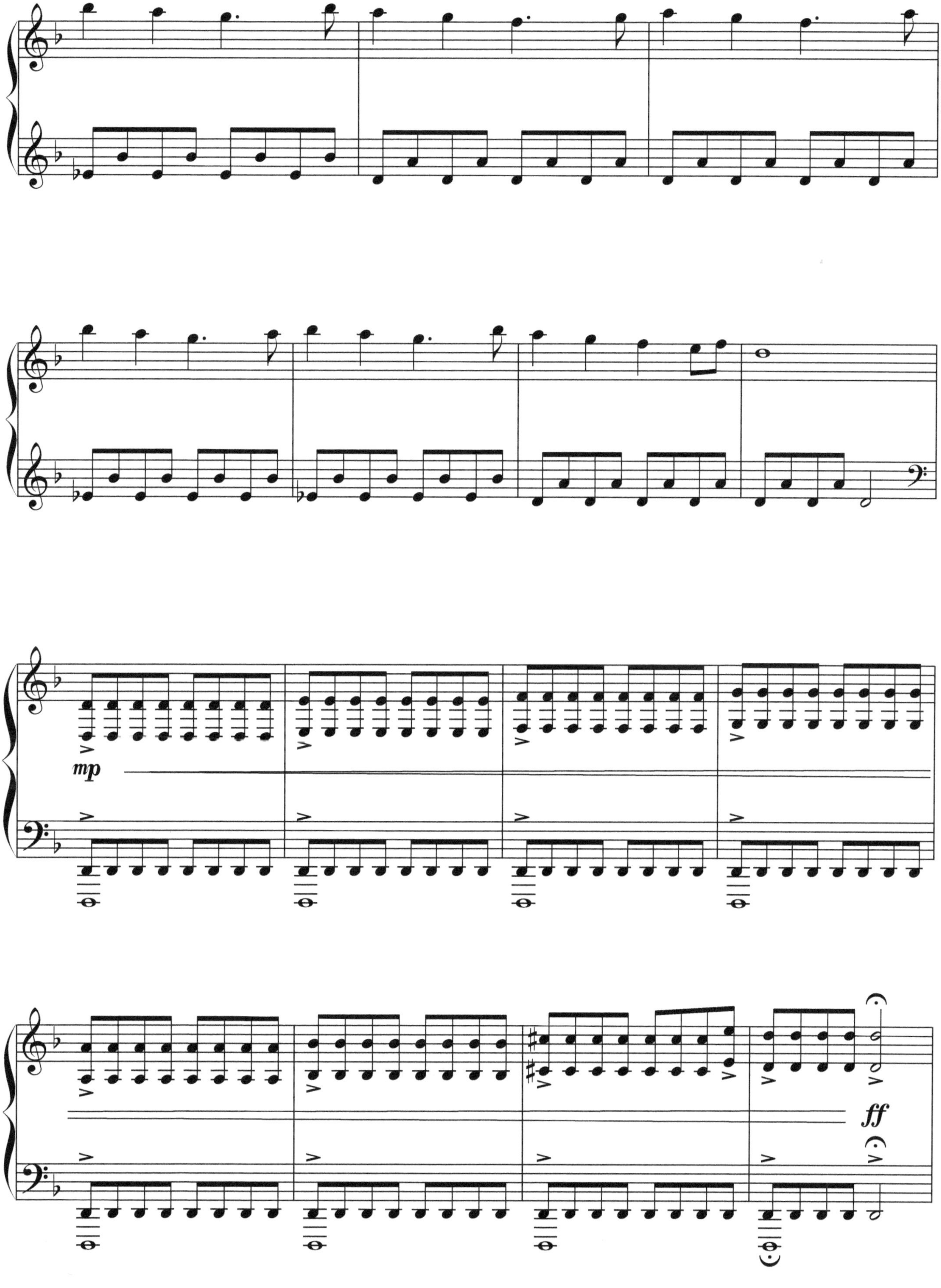
mp
ff

Quite Fast, Intense ♩ = 192

A little slower ♩ = 148

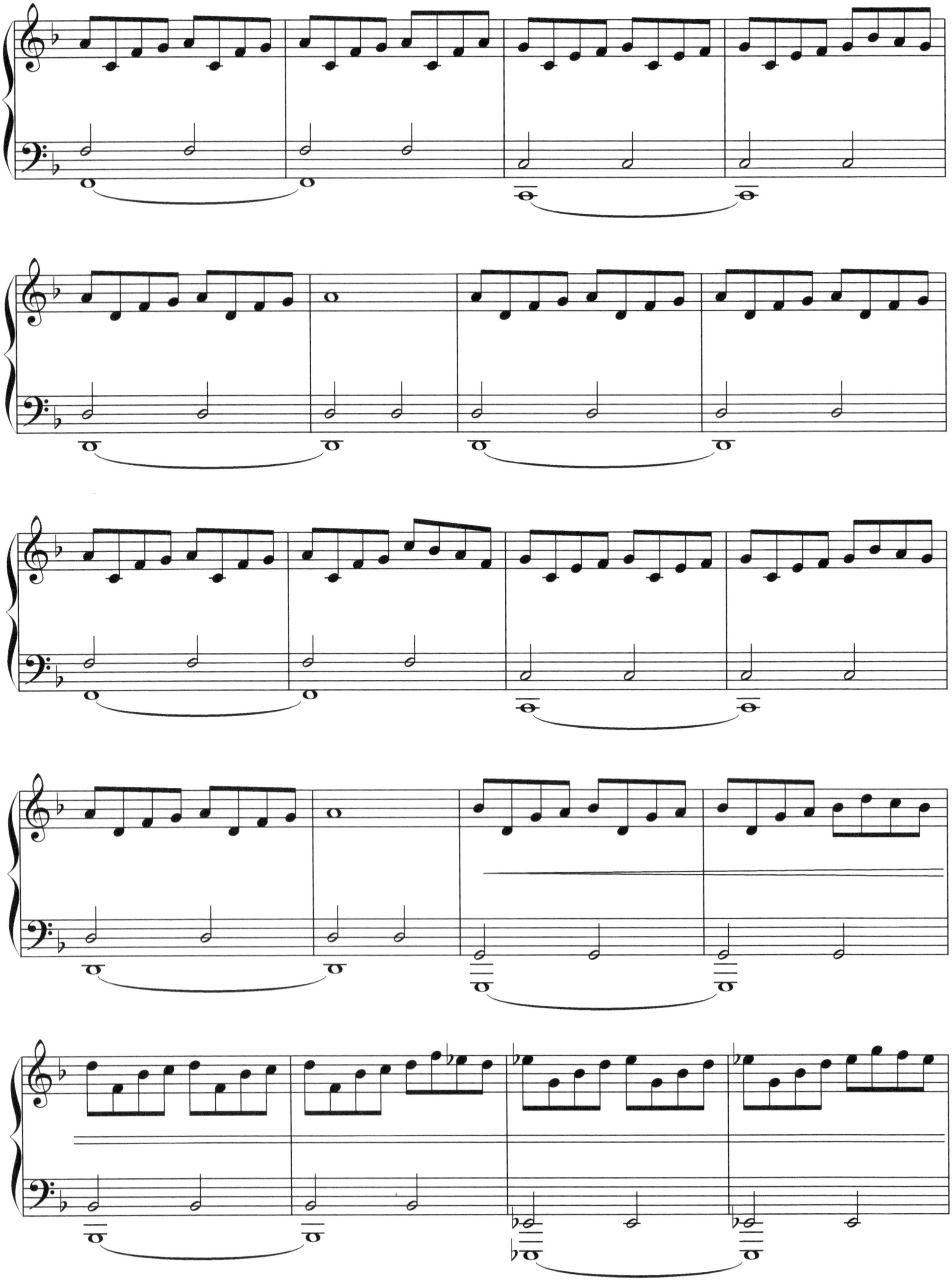

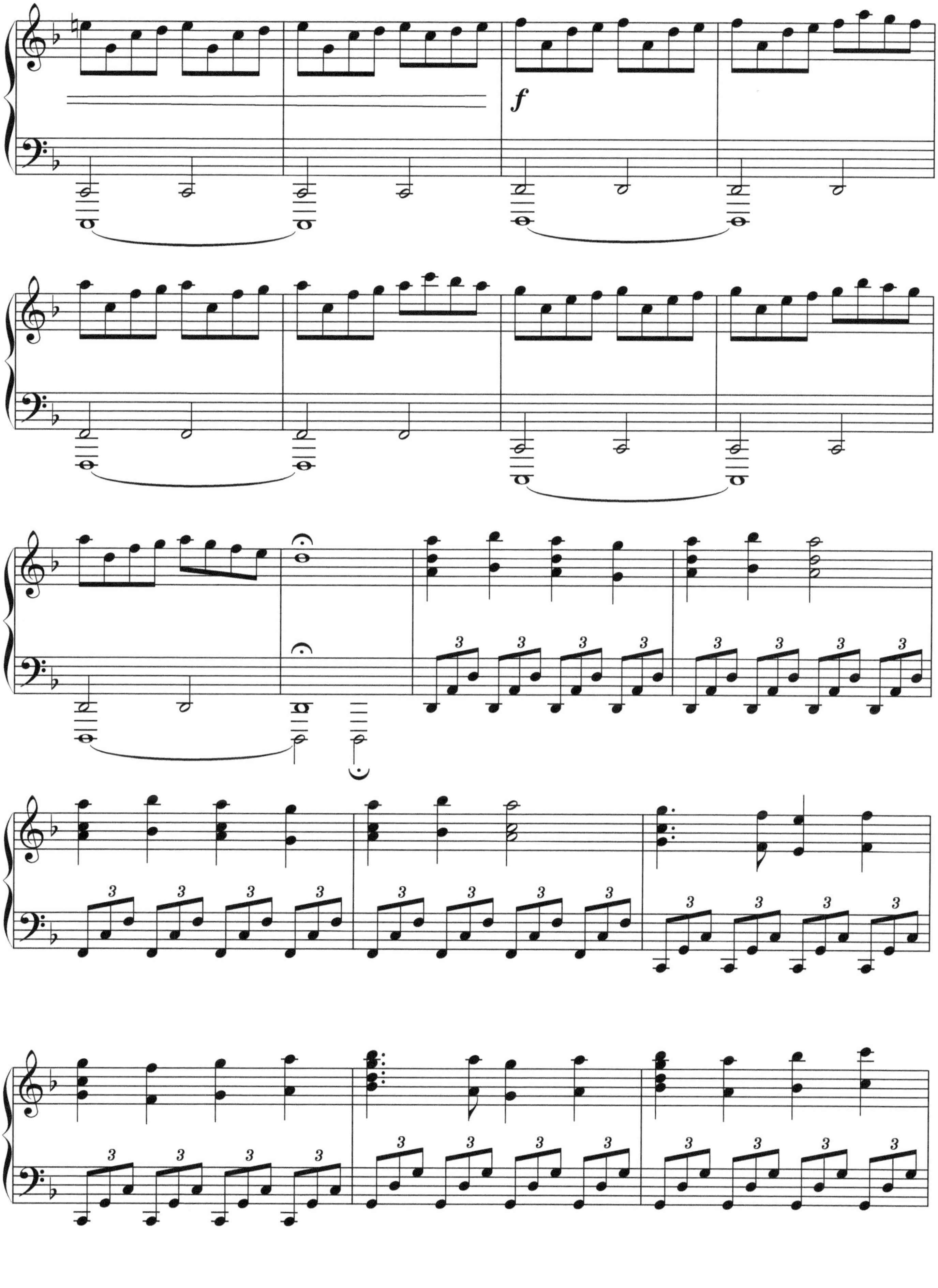
f
3

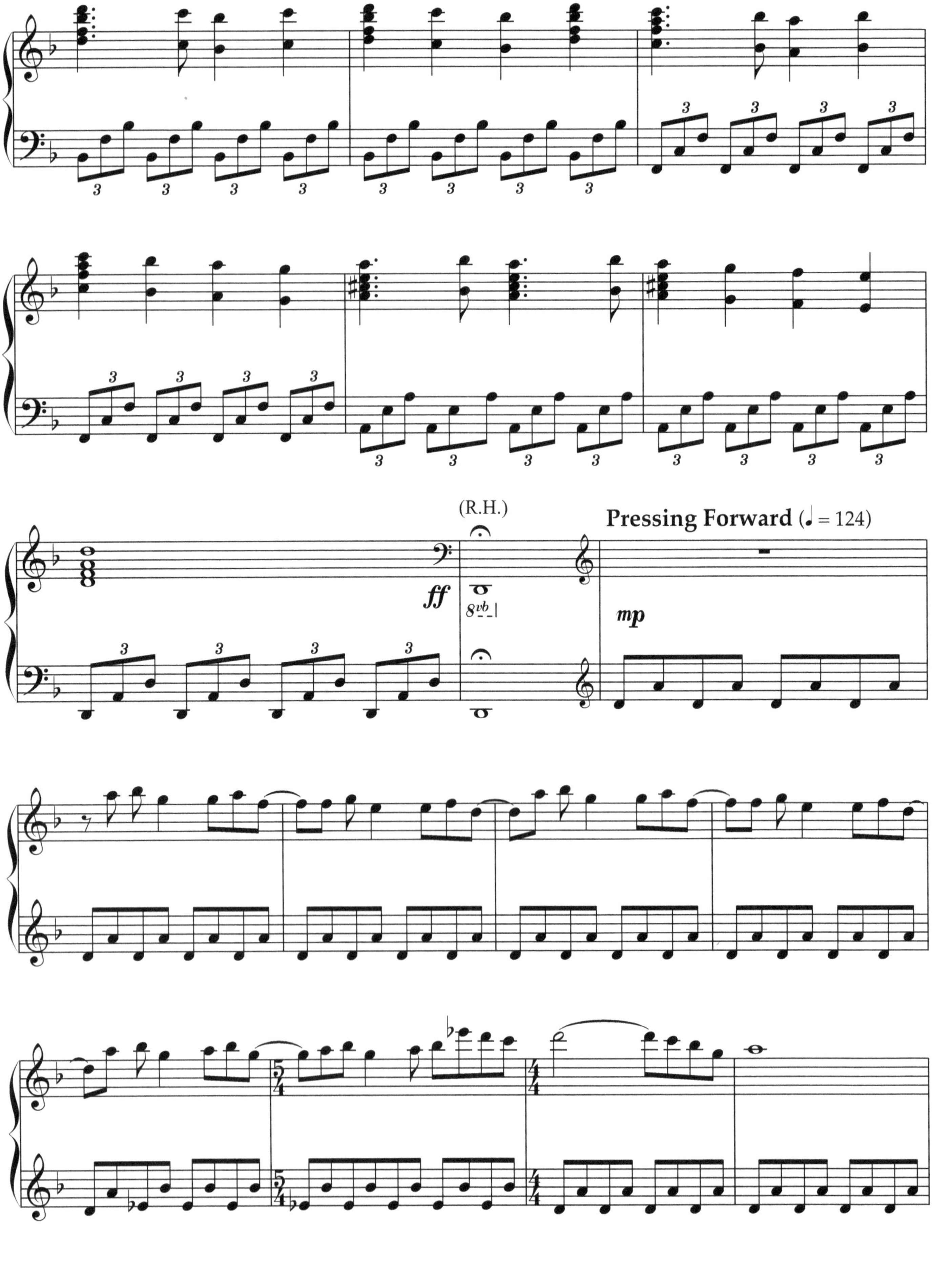
3
ff
(R.H.)
8vb
Pressing Forward (♩ = 124)
mp
5
4
4
4

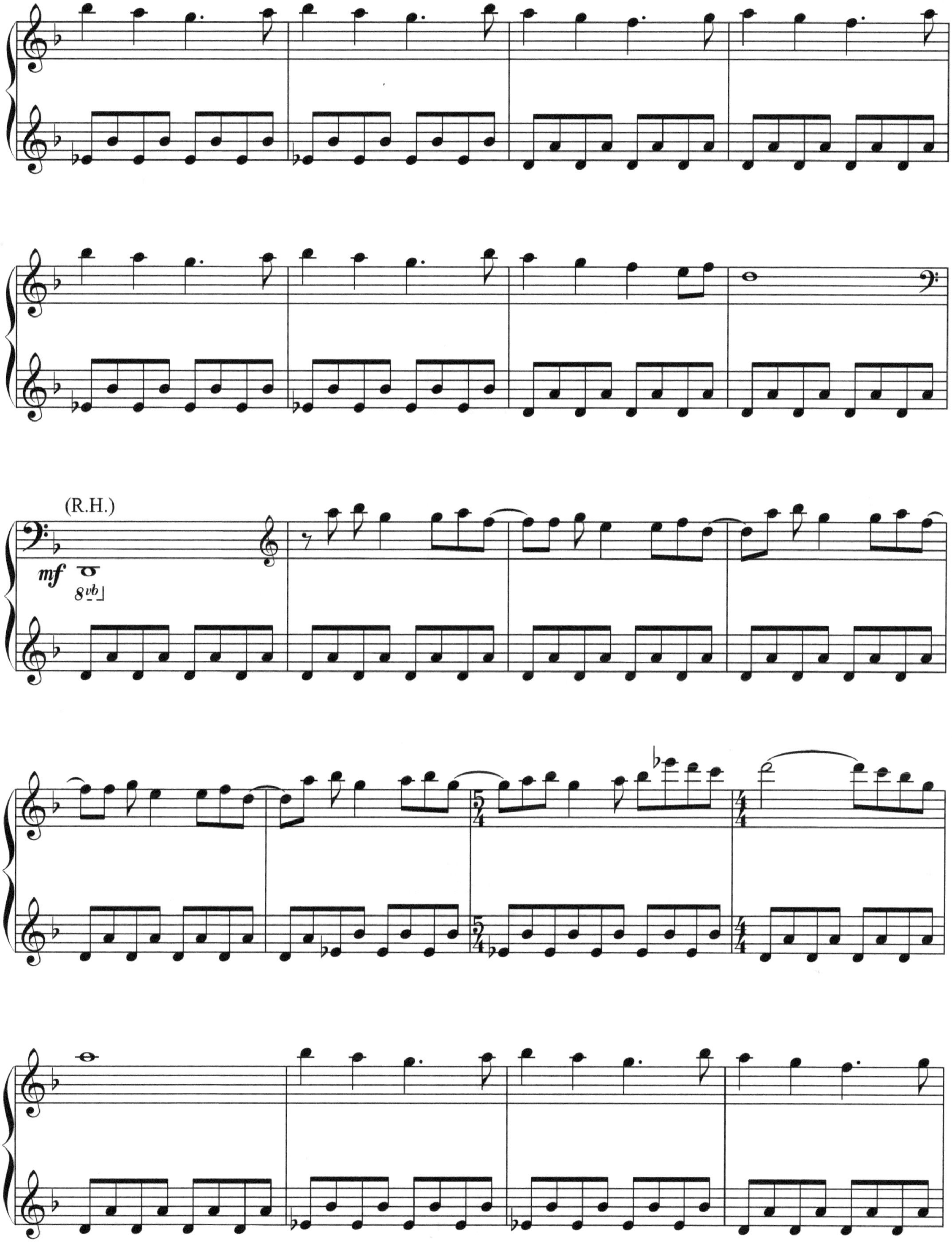
(R.H.)
mf
8vb

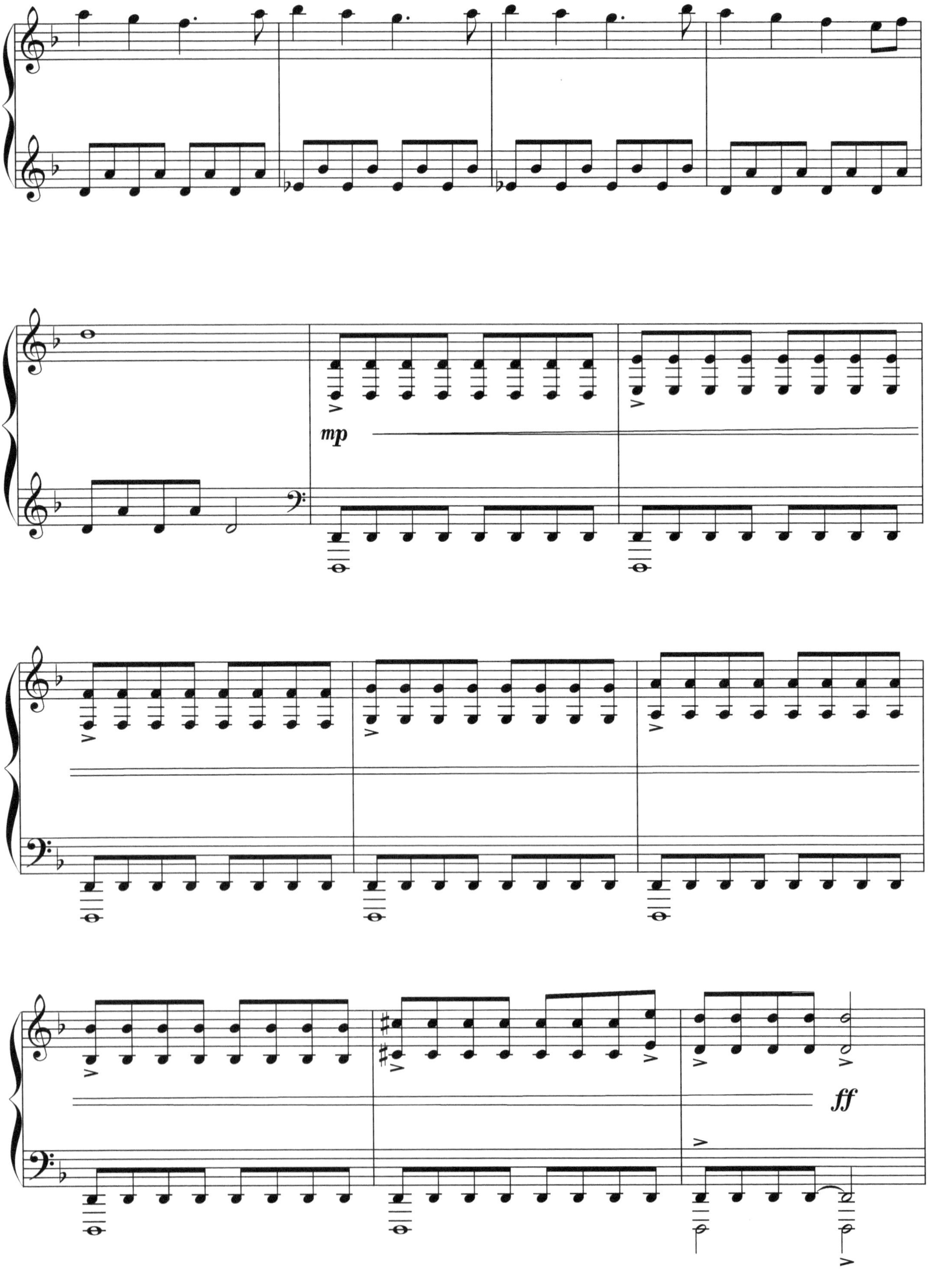
mp
ff

Determined ($\quarter$ = 136)

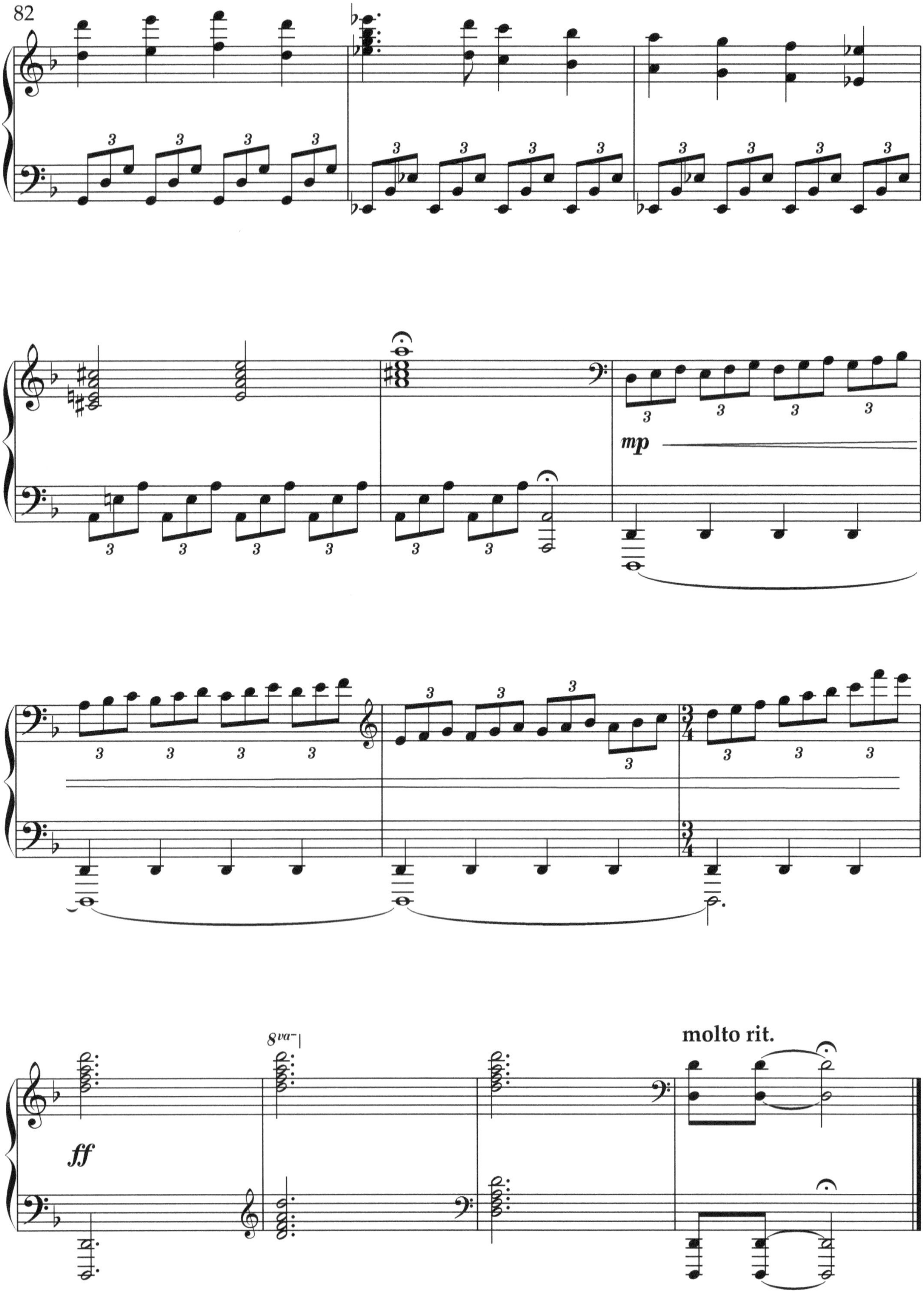
82
mp
ff
8va
molto rit.

For Angie

Music by Bill Walker

Tempo rubato, with feeling (♪ = 164 - 180)

With pedal

molto rit.

Faster (♪ = 192 - 208)

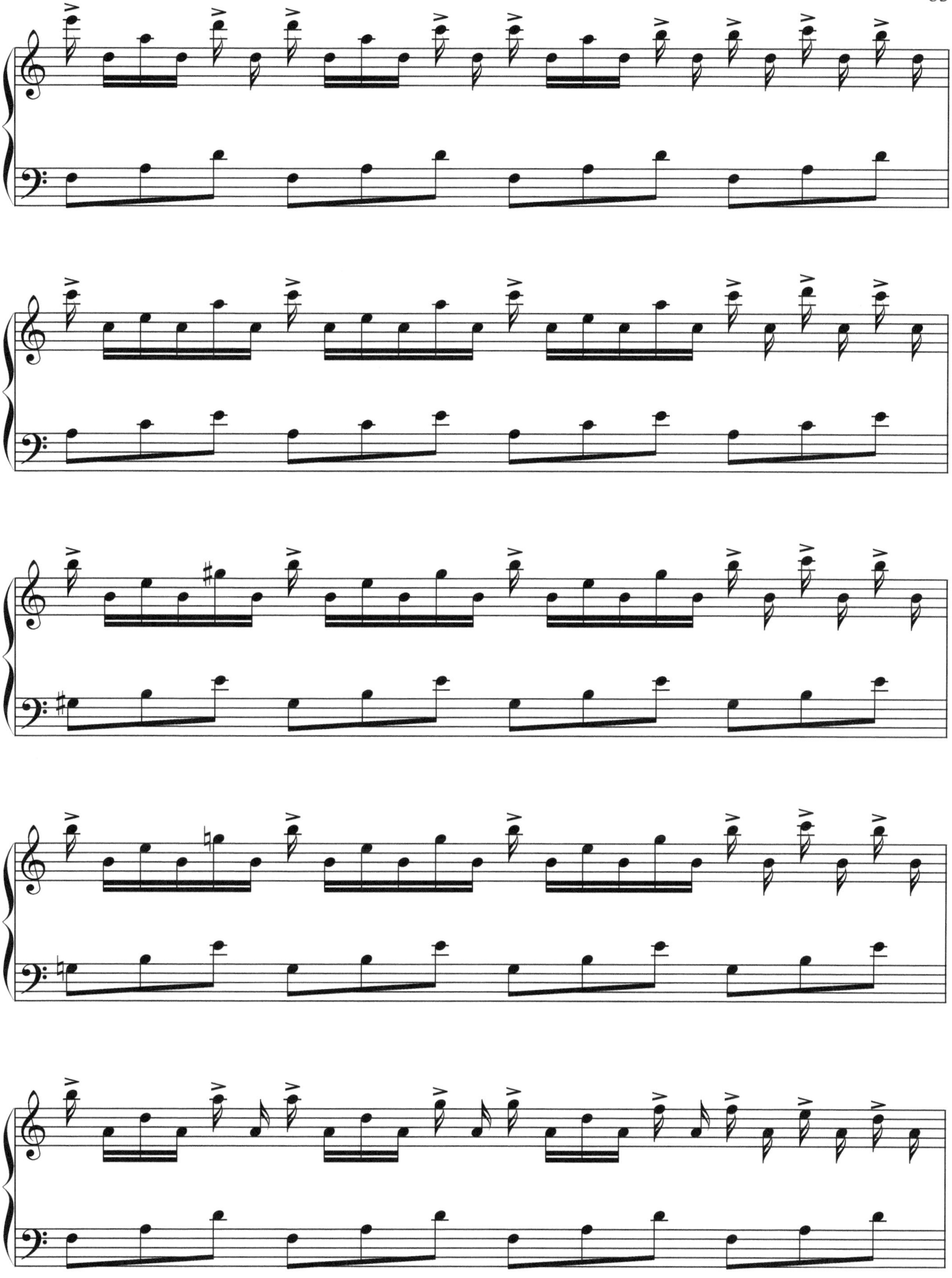

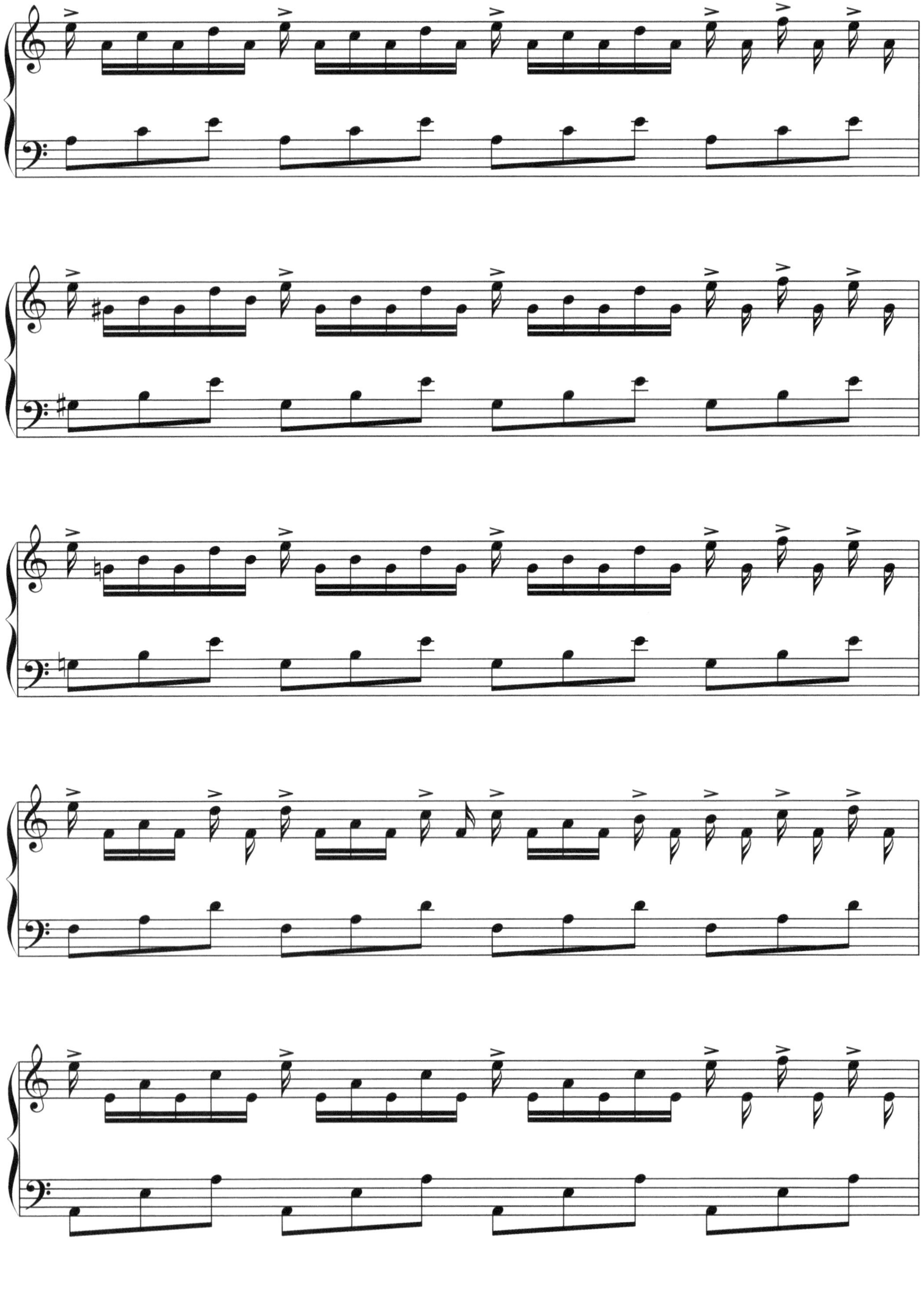

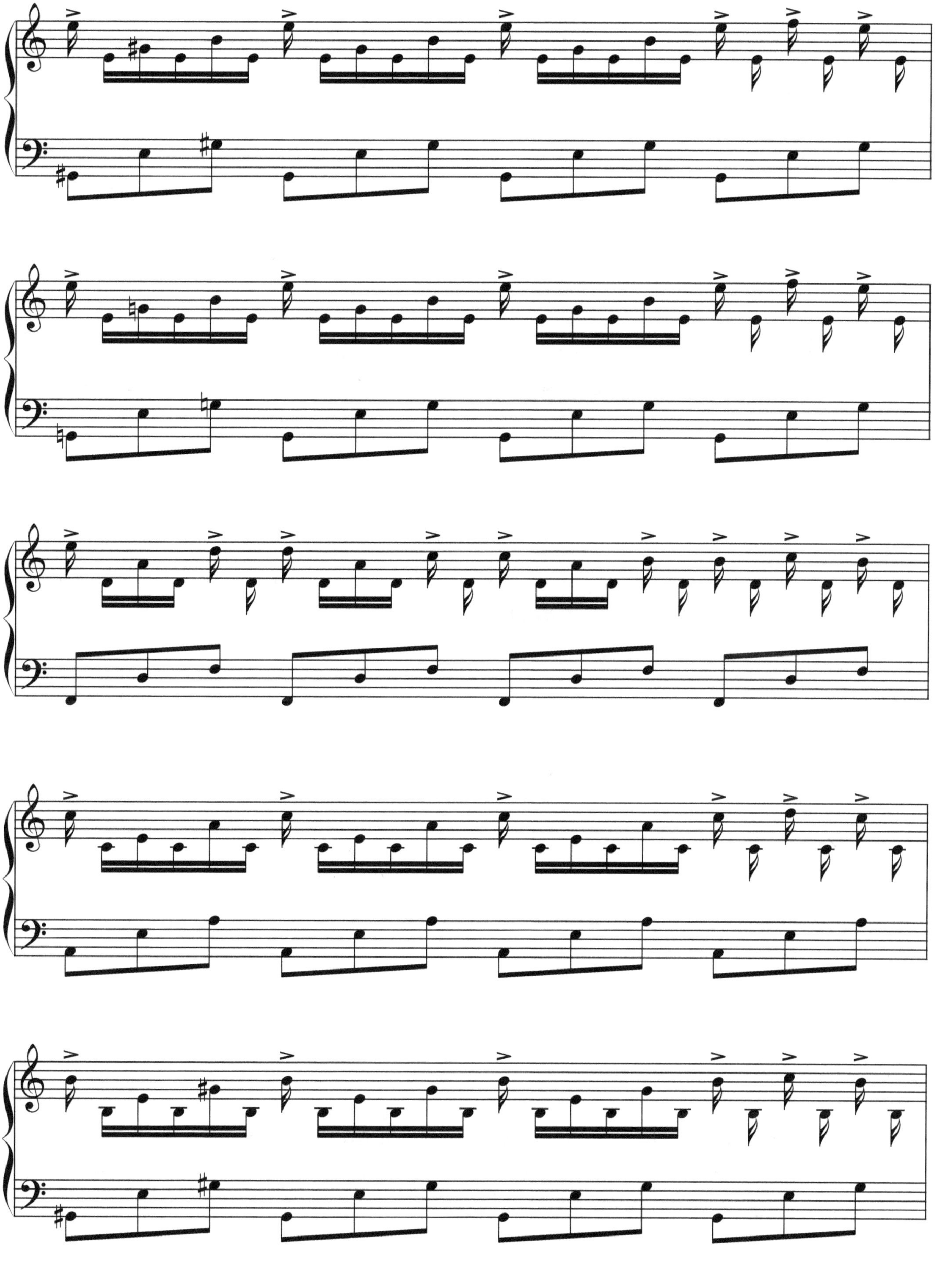

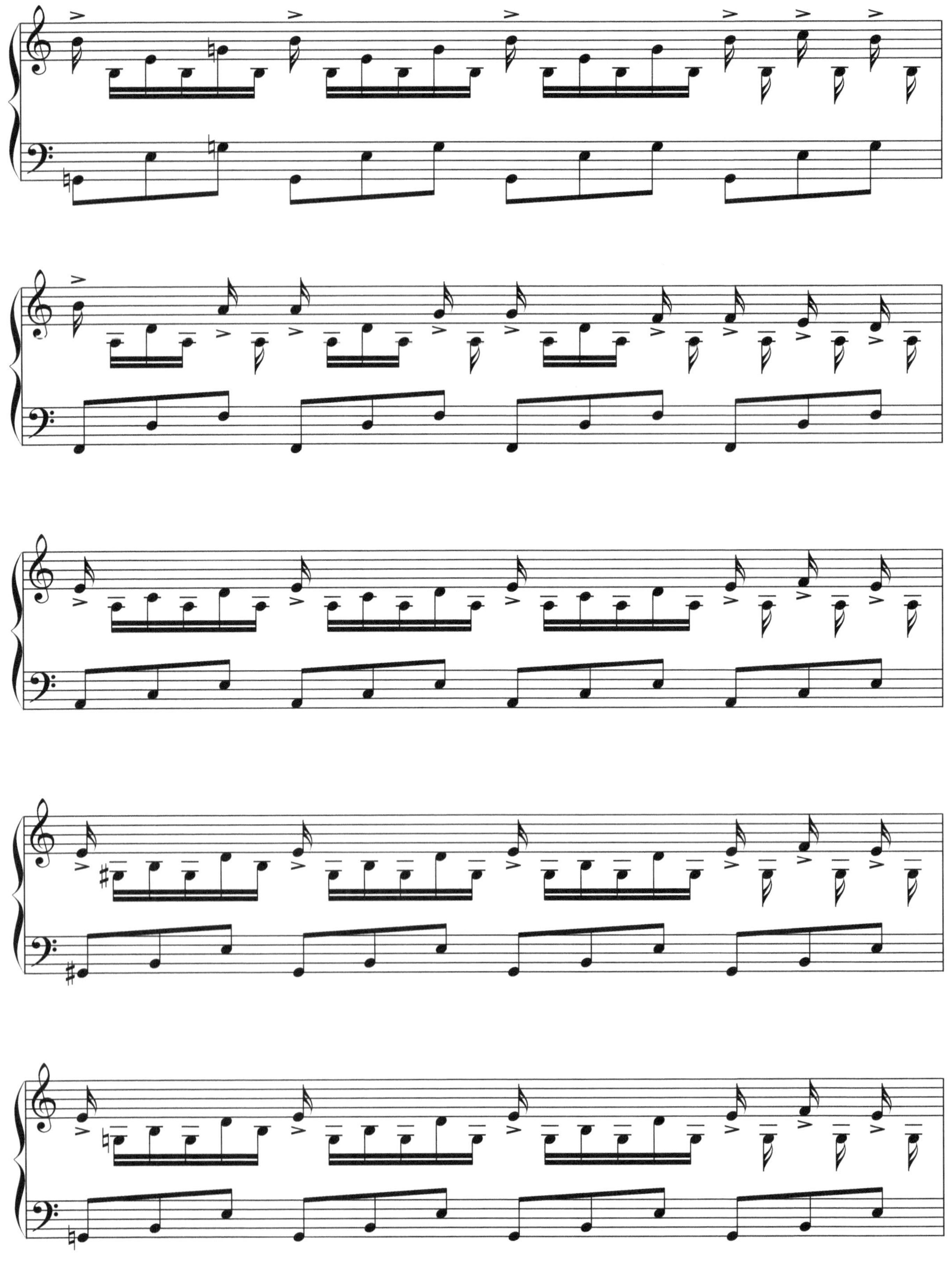

rit. _ _ _ _ _ _ _ _

Tempo primo (♪ = 164 - 180)

mp

mf

molto rit.

Faster (♪ = 192 - 208)

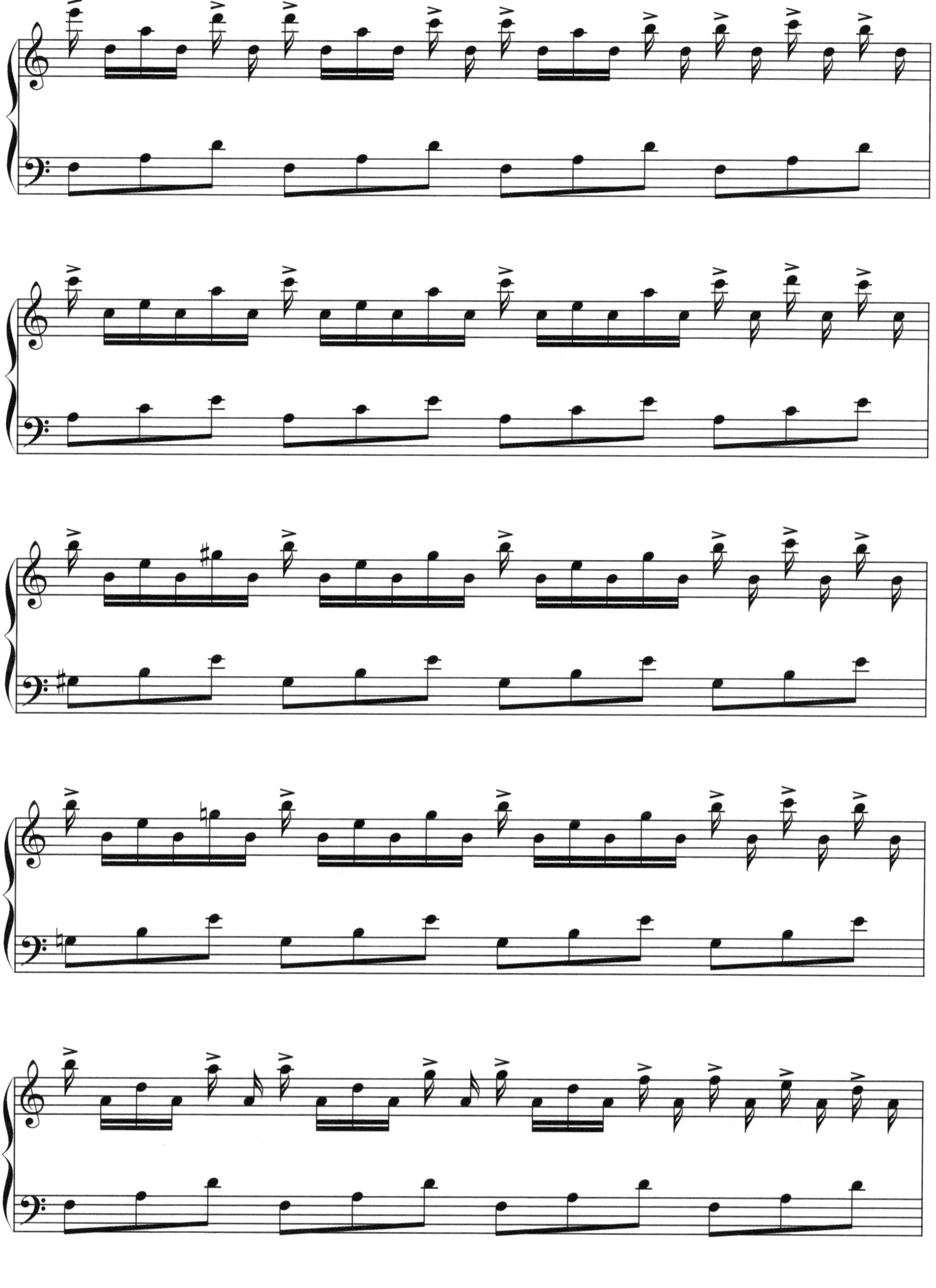

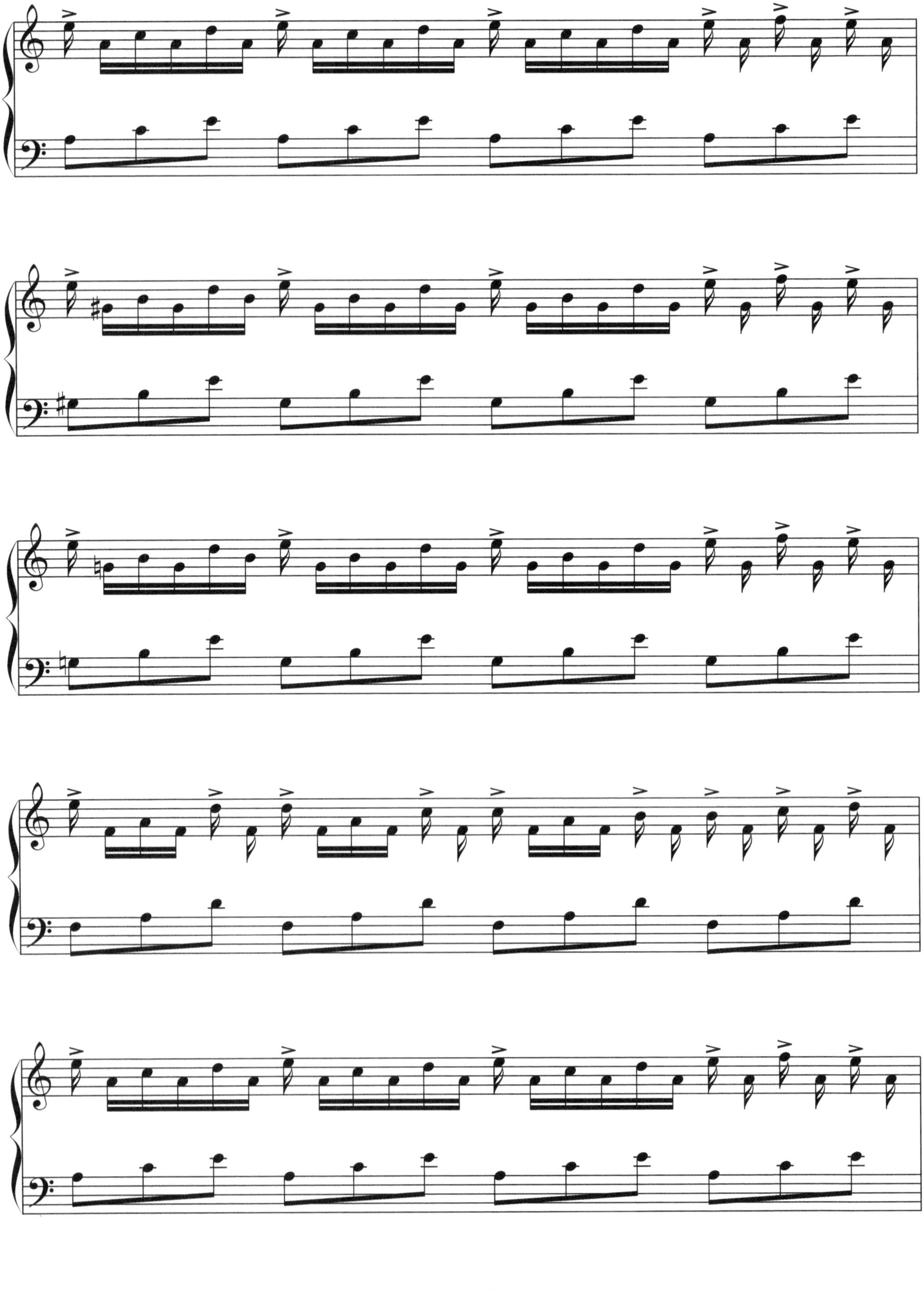

Tempo primo ($\flat$ = 164 - 180)

mp

rit. - - - - - - - - - - - - - -

(R.H.)

p

Other books by Bill Walker Music Publishing

Mastery of Keys: A Comprehensive Guide of Scales, Arpeggios, and Chords
Published: 2023

The Joy of Christmas
Published: 2023

Reverie
Published: 2024

Paperback available at Amazon
eBook and individual titles available at Sheet Music Plus & my website

Visit my website:

www.billwalkercomposer.com

Join my free Facebook group for Passionate Piano Composers:

www.facebook.com/groups/pianocomposers

www.ingramcontent.com/pod-product-compliance
Lightning Source LLC
Chambersburg PA
CBHW062050090426
42740CB00016B/3082